Ottoman Empire
and Islamic
Tradition

STUDIES IN
WORLD CIVILIZATION
Consulting Editor:
Eugene Rice
Columbia University

Ottoman Empire and Islamic Tradition

NORMAN ITZKOWITZ
Princeton University

Alfred A. Knopf   *New York*

THIS IS A BORZOI BOOK
PUBLISHED BY ALFRED A. KNOPF, INC.

Library of Congress Cataloging in Publication Data

Itzkowitz, Norman, 1931–   , Ottoman Empire and
Islamic tradition.
(Studies in world civilization)
Bibliography: p.
1. Turkey—History. 2. Islam—Turkey.
I. Title. II. Series.
DR445.I8 949.6 72–1914
ISBN 0–394–31718–1

Manufactured in the United States of America

First Edition

9 8 7 6 5 4 3 2 1

Typography and cover design by Elton Robinson.
Cover map by J. P. Tremblay.

Preface

This book provides the student with an introduction to the historical development of the Ottoman Empire and an appreciation of its institutions, social structure, and intellectual foundations. The narrative carries the Ottomans from their beginning on the Byzantine frontier as an Islamic warrior principality, through the development of their empire, down to the late eighteenth century when they found it necessary to embark upon the process of modernization. I have delineated the fundamental institutions of the Ottoman state, the major dividing lines within the society, and the basic ideas on government and social structure that helped the Ottomans found their empire, fostered its growth, and then sustained it through periods of internal dissension and external threat.

Patterning the fabric of Ottoman existence in all its manifestations was the High Islamic tradition in government and society. That tradition had been mediated to the Ottomans through the Seljuks of Rum who had preceded them in Anatolia. Entailing orthodoxy in religious matters, fiscal policies characterized by their differential treatment of Muslims and non-Muslims, a military establishment supported largely by feudal grants, an administrative-military elite of slaves trained in the service of the sultan, and a class structure that divided society into legally privileged and non-privileged, the High Islamic tradition provided the modality through which the Ottomans experienced the world and interacted with it.

Latecomers as the Ottomans were in the chronology of Islam, there was still room for them to contribute to the inherited tradition and mold it with their own particular genius for administration and government. Their innovations and refinements include the levy of young male Christian subjects for the slave household and military establishment, the palace school with its system of promotions and interlocking relationship with the administration of the external real world through the graduation process, and the elaboration of the social structure along functional lines.

The emphasis in this work is on how the Ottomans viewed their historical experience, what they thought about their society, how they conceptualized their problems, and their own attempts at problem-solving. I have sought to let the Ottomans speak for themselves. In this way we can penetrate beyond the surface view provided by the insights of Western observers of the Ottoman world to the core of Ottoman existence.

I have had to be selective in the events described and topics treated, for it is manifestly impossible to cover five hundred years of history fully within the confines of so short a book. The stress is on the sweep and grandeur of Ottoman history just to the point when the impact of the West would begin to be felt in the Near East. I hope this work will provide insights into how another culture dealt with the problems of government and society, as well as with those of greatness and decline.

In the course of writing this book, I have drawn upon the research of many of my colleagues in the field. I wish to thank them all, and to acknowledge a special debt to the work of Claude Cahen, Halil Inalcik, Bernard Lewis, Geoffrey L. Lewis, Victor Menagè, Lewis V. Thomas, Dorothy Vaughan, and Paul Wittek. I am indebted to them for the insights they provided and for the inspiration of their example. The act of synthesizing my own views with the body of accumulated wisdom proved to be a most enjoyable experience. I am most grateful to Geoffrey L. Lewis who read the manuscript and made valuable suggestions, and to John W. Shy for his encouragement.

N. I.
Princeton, New Jersey

March, 1972

Contents

Introduction   xi

Chapter 1   From Emirate to Empire   3
            Turkish Migration   4
            Seljuks   5
            Seljuks of Rum   8
            The Emirate of Osman   10
            Orhon   11
            Ottoman Methods of Conquest   13
            Bajazet the Thunderbolt   16
            Bajazet's Legacy   20
            Recovery and Renewed Conquest   21
            Mohammed the Conqueror   24
            Istanbul   27
            Bajazet II   29
            Selim the Grim   32
            Suleiman the Magnificent   34

Chapter 2   Ottoman Society and Institutions   37
            Steppe, Ghazi, and Class   38
            Askeris and *Reaya*   40
            Timars and Timar-holders   40
            Provincial Structure   41
            Provincial Administration   47
            The *Ghulam* System   49
            The Grand Vizier and the Divan   54
            The Bureaucracy   55
            Justice   57
            The True Ottomans   59

Social Mobility   60

Chapter 3   The Post-Suleimanic Age   63
The Muscovy Menace   63
Conflict in North Africa   65
Conflict in the East   68
Conflict in the West   71
Back to the East   72
Ottoman Succession   74
Sultanate of the Women   75
The Kuprili Era   77
Second Siege of Vienna   81
Aftermath of 1683   82

Chapter 4   Ottoman Consciousness   87
The Circle of Equity   88
Disruption in the Timar System   89
Expansion of the Janissary Corps   90
Sekbans and *Celâlîs*   92
Causes   93
The Kuprili Era in Perspective   99
The Historian Naima   100
The Medical Analogy   101
Eighteenth-Century Success   103
Ottoman Knowledge of Europe   104
Success Breeds Failure   107
The Ottoman-Russian War   108
Selim III   108

Bibliography   111

Chronology   115

Glossary   117

Index   follows page 118

Introduction

Professor Itzkowitz's essay on the Ottoman Empire is one in a series of twelve paperbacks that Alfred A. Knopf, Inc., is publishing under the title *Studies in World Civilization*. A second study will be devoted to medieval Islam. Of the ten other studies in the series, one book·deals with early and one with modern developments in Africa, China, India, Japan, and Latin America. The purposes of the series are to introduce students early in their careers to the historical experience of peoples, societies, and civilizations different from their own; to provide a core of attractive readings for courses in World Civilization; and, at the same time, to furnish teachers of Western Civilization with comparative evidence from non-Western history deliberately selected to illuminate central problems in the Western historical experience.

One of the intellectual virtues of our time is a willingness to recognize both the relativism of our own past and present beliefs and the civilizing value of the study of alien cultures. Yet, in practice, as every teaching historian knows, it is immensely difficult to construct a viable course in world history; and almost as difficult to include satisfactorily unfamiliar, and especially non-Western, materials in the traditional Western Civilization survey course. The reason for this difficulty is that until very recently mankind had no common past. The pre-Columbian civilizations of America attained their splendor in total isolation from the rest of the world. Although the many different ancient peoples living around the Mediterranean were often in close touch with one another, they had little knowledge about civilizations elsewhere. The Chinese knew accurately no other high civilization. Until the nineteenth century, they regarded the ideals of their own culture as normative for the entire world. Medieval Europe, despite fruitful contact with the Islamic world, was a closed society;

medieval Western historians identified their own past with the history of the human race and gave it meaning and value by believing that this past was the expression of a providential plan.

The fifteenth-century European voyages of discovery began a new era in the relations between Europe and the rest of the world. Between 1500 and 1900, Europeans displaced the populations of three other continents, conquered India, partitioned Africa, and decisively influenced the historical development of China and Japan. The expansion of Europe over the world gave Western historians a unifying theme: the story of how the non-Western world became the economic hinterland, political satellite, and technological debtor of Europe. Despite an enormously increased knowledge of the religions, arts and literatures, social structures, and political institutions of non-Western peoples, Western historians wrote a universal history that remained radically provincial. Only their assumptions changed. Before 1500, these assumptions were theological; by the nineteenth century, they were indistinguishable from those of intelligent colonial governors.

The decline of European dominance, the rise to power of hitherto peripheral Western countries such as the United States and the Soviet Union and of non-Western ones such as China and Japan, and the emergence of a world economy and a state system embracing the planet have all created further options and opened wider perspectives. Historians of the future will be able to write real world history because for good and ill the world has begun to live a single history; and while this makes it no easier than before to understand and write the history of the world's remoter past, contemporary realities and urgencies have widened our curiosity and enlarged our sympathies and made less provincial our notions of what is relevant to us in the world's past.

One viable way to overcome the ethnocentric provincialism of an exclusively Western perspective is to deal with both Western and non-Western civilizations on a comparative basis. The comparative procedure has a double advantage. On the one hand, it describes a culture different from our own and makes clear to us that in order to understand it we must scan its history with humility and sophistication, abandoning implicit analogies with our own civilization and leaving aside some of our most fundamental assumptions about time, space, causality, and even about human nature itself. On the other hand, it encourages us to make explicit those very assumptions of our own tradition we now recognize to be different or unique. By studying comparatively an alien civilization we learn something about it—a good in itself—and at the same time sharpen our understanding of ourselves.

Professor Itzkowitz's book serves these purposes admirably. It is a splendid analysis of the social structure, political institutions, and ideas of a non-Western people whose capital was founded by a Roman emperor and whose empire included a large part of Europe. The Ottomans were Muslims and the inheritors of the classic Islamic civilization. By the sixteenth century their empire was also an integral part of the European state system. Their history therefore combines the familiar and unfamiliar in fascinatingly complex and instructive ways. Few societies, for example, offer more copious and more interesting data about slavery than the Ottoman. The sultan's elite infantry, the famous janissaries, were slaves. Able slaves received the finest education in the Islamic world and occupied the highest posts in the administration of the state, including that of grand vizier. Clearly slavery played a different role among the Ottomans than it played in Western Europe. It is equally interesting to compare the European patterns of aggression and the European justifications for aggression with the bellicosity of the Ottoman state, whose explicit guiding purpose was the holy war against the infidel; to note the differences between the European fief and the way the sultans supported the warrior aristocrats with the use and revenue of land in return for service as heavy cavalry; and to observe how differently the idea of an empire was embodied at one end of the Mediterranean Sea by Charles V and at the other end by Suleiman the Magnificent. By the end of this study Professor Itzkowitz has taught the reader the most valuable and interesting lesson of all: to look at both the Ottomans and Europeans through Ottoman eyes and to see the world from an Ottoman perspective.

EUGENE RICE
Columbia University

Ottoman Empire and Islamic Tradition

Chapter 1

From Emirate
to Empire

Constantinople, like Rome, is a city of hills and was the capital of the eastern Roman world. After the Ottomans conquered that capital in 1453, they took advantage of nature's gifts and crowned the hills with monumental mosques, making the silhouette of Istanbul one of the world's most breath-taking urban sights. Once seen, its image is indelibly stamped upon the memory. Nedim, the eighteenth-century Ottoman lyric poet, extolled the city's glories:

Stambul, peerless of cities, thou jewel beyond compare,
Seated astride upon two seas, with dazzling light aflare!
One single stone of thine, me thinks, of greater worth by far than
    all the treasures of Iran!
Resplendent as the Sun whose rays the world in light enshrine.
Thy gardens, visions of delight, patterns of Joy Divine,
Thy shady nooks of rosebeds fair, of Love's enchantments full,
    challenge the Prophet's Paradise.*

Fittingly ensconced on Stambul's highest hill is the

---

*Quoted in Alexander Pallis, *In the Days of the Janissaries* (London: Hutchinson and Company Ltd., 1951), p. 69.

3

majestic mosque of Suleiman, the loftiness of its dome taking second place only to that of Hagia Sophia (Holy Wisdom). Completed in 1557, that mosque was created by the master architect Sinan Pasha upon the order of Sultan Suleiman. It has four minarets with ten galleries from which the muezzins can call the faithful to prayer. Numbers in the mystical East are seldom without special meaning. The ten and the four symbolize milestones in the dynasty's heroic history. Suleiman was the tenth sultan in the family line and the fourth Ottoman to rule over the peerless city since its conquest in 1453 by Mohammed II.

Suleiman reigned over the sprawling Ottoman Empire during the Renaissance, a contemporary of Charles V, Francis I, and Henry VIII, each of whom was the representative of a proud line, but none more proud than the Ottoman. As the tenth Ottoman sultan, Suleiman could take pride in the fact that few dynasties in world history had such a long and almost unbroken succession of remarkable rulers.

TURKISH
MIGRATION

The first of these remarkable rulers was Osman, the eponymous founder of the dynasty, who is said to have reigned from 1299 to 1326. There is no need to give in detail the complicated history of the migrations of the Oghuz confederation of Turkish tribes from Central Asia to Asia Minor that ultimately gave rise to the House of Osman. It is sufficient to note that in the tenth century those indomitable steppe peoples were located in an area of Central Asia bounded in the south by the Aral Sea and the lower course of the Syr Darya (Jaxartes) River, in the west by the Caspian Sea and the lower Volga River, and in the northeast by the Irtysh River. They were largely nomadic, their wealth consisting of camels, horses, and sheep. Some settled groups raised crops in the oases and bartered in market towns, exchanging animals, forest products (mostly furs), and captives for goods from the urban areas to the south and west along the Muslim border. Those economic contacts with Muslims facilitated the conversion of the Oghuz Turks to the Muslim faith.

Islam succeeded among the Turks where Buddhism,

Manicheanism, and Judaism had failed. It began to make inroads against their ancestral shamanism early in the tenth century. Contacts with Muslims were primarily of three sorts: raiders encountered in skirmishes along the southern border (and the prisoners taken by both sides), wandering Muslim holy men (Sufis and dervishes), and merchants. The commercial contacts appear to have been the most influential in the long process of conversion. By the end of the tenth century Islam was securely established among the Oghuz Turks, who were now separated from the Islamic territories to the south only by the Syr Darya River.

SELJUKS   Once converted to Islam, the Turks began a southward expansion across that river under the leadership of the Seljuk family. The Seljuks started as military bands hired by Muslim princes and soon emerged as governors of provinces and eventually became autonomous rulers of vast areas. After overrunning Persia (Isfahan fell in 1043), the Seljuks struck out in a westerly direction. Under the leadership of Tughrul Beg, they thrust themselves into the settled centers of classical High Islam. Baghdad, the seat of the caliphate, fell in 1055.

The Seljuks, deriving their strength from the possession of both a force of regulars and an army of nomads, created a new empire in the Islamic heartland. Although they were in the service of the caliphs, who remained the supreme religious leaders, the Seljuk sultans wielded power independently in the name of Islam. Soon the conquerors were themselves conquered by the Persian-Islamic traditions of their new homeland. In religious matters the Seljuks came to champion orthodoxy, and in governmental and social organization they relied upon the traditional patterns of the civilization of classical Islam. Based upon Islamic principles of taxation, the Seljuk regime was sustained by a military class supported through land grants in return for service and functioned in behalf of the military, bureaucratic, and religious aristocracy.

This aristocracy, however, was threatened by the Islamized nomadic Turks known as the Turcomans. The unruly

Turcomans abhorred the civilization of High Islam since it was identified in their minds with the dual evils of taxation and religious orthodoxy. They were impelled by the love of booty and the desire to spread the faith of the Prophet Muhammad, and they preferred the freer atmosphere of the frontier where they could more easily satisfy their yearnings for loot and independence. The Seljuks encouraged the Turcomans and other tribal elements to raid and plunder the eastern provinces of the Byzantine Empire in Anatolia in order to divert them from settled Islamic areas. The Turcomans swelled the ranks of the Muslim frontier warriors already engaged in combat against the Byzantines. These warriors, who inhabited the military borderland between Byzantium and Islam, were known as ghazis, or warriors for the faith. The sacred duty of the ghazi was to extend the Islamic territory (darülislâm, "Abode of Islam") at the expense of the land inhabited by the non-Muslims (darülharb, "Abode of War"). He did this by means of the ghaza, or raid, which came to be the perpetual warfare carried on against unbelievers, especially Christians. Wealth captured in this type of warfare was, according to the religious law of Islam, the sharia, lawful booty, and the inhabitants of the raided area could be enslaved or massacred.

As the number of ghazis on the frontier increased, their raids became more frequent and venturesome, penetrating deeper into the Byzantine Empire in Anatolia. In 1064 their incursions carried them as far as Ani and Caesarea (modern Kayseri). Those successes provoked a military response from Constantinople. Romanus IV Diogenes, a member of the Byzantine military nobility, became emperor in 1068. He replaced Constantine Ducas, who had been a representative of the bureaucratic establishment in the capital and whose financial and religious policies had allowed the frontier situation to degenerate. The new emperor carried the battle to the ghazis with renewed vigor and success.

The Byzantines were so successful that the Seljuk sultan, Alp Arslan, was compelled to march into Anatolia at the head of his army. Direct confrontation was contrary to

Seljuk policy. Alp Arslan had hoped to avoid a clash with Byzantium on the northwestern frontier in order to concentrate his military strength on expansion in Syria and Palestine. Nevertheless, in August 1071 the Seljuks routed the Byzantines at Manzikert near Lake Van. Anatolia was now open to full-scale invasion and permanent settlement, and the long process of Anatolia's Turkification and Islamization was set in motion.

Conquest and settlement were accomplished not by the regular Seljuk army, which withdrew following the victory at Manzikert, but rather by the ghazis. Under the direction of a number of chiefs, such as Danishmend and Ahmed Ghazi, who demonstrated the personal qualities necessary for success in the dangerous and hostile frontier environment, the warriors for the faith began to wrest control of Anatolia from Byzantine hands. This process was facilitated by the internal confusion and anarchy in Byzantium that followed the defeat at Manzikert. The border regions rose in rebellion, and the Byzantine defense system collapsed. Faced with little organized resistance, the ghazis were successful, and each success attracted more ghazis to the expanding frontier.

Ghazis, however, were not the only ones attracted to Anatolia. The Seljuk government decided to incorporate under its own control all the newly conquered regions of Anatolia, although it was not yet committed to expansion into Anatolia. The government sent Suleiman ibn Kutulmush, a prince of the ruling house, to govern. His father had lost his life in a rebellion against the head of the dynasty, and posting the son to Anatolia would rid the dynasty of an undesirable. For his part, Suleiman saw the assignment as an opportunity to establish a firm base of personal support. He hoped to build an army among the Turcomans, march eastward against the centers of the Muslim world under the control of his relatives, and claim them for his own.

Suleiman took control of Nicaea (modern Iznik) in 1081 and negotiated with the Byzantine government, which expected him to keep the Turcomans under control in return for the right to settle his troops in the conquered areas. Byzantine administration was quickly superseded in a vast part of Anatolia, although nominally Suleiman recognized Byzantine suzerainty. The exile to Anatolia then felt strong enough to turn his attention to his primary objective, the central Muslim world. Suleiman marched against Aleppo but met with strong opposition and was killed in battle in 1086, and his army retreated into Anatolia.

SELJUKS OF RUM   Suleiman's death brought no major change in policy. Not until the middle of the twelfth century did the descendants of Suleiman ibn Kutulmush begin to look upon Anatolia as the area in which they would carve out a kingdom for themselves rather than as a staging ground for their return to the central Muslim world. Finally they focused their energies on the central Anatolian steppe around the city of Iconium (modern Konya) and founded a kingdom known as Rum. ("Rum" was the Muslim term used to designate the Asian provinces of the Roman Empire ruled over by the Byzantines.)

From their center at Konya, the Seljuks of Rum carried on a twofold struggle for expansion. They did battle in central Anatolia with their rivals the Danishmends and carried on the holy war against the crusaders. The Danishmends typified the older ghazi spirit of frontier warfare; they had created an eclectic culture infused with mysticism, heterodoxy, and tribal customs. The Seljuks of Rum represented the governmental and cultural traditions of High Islam; they desired a Muslim principality characterized by sound administration, political integration, orthodoxy, and culture. Thus the two were unalterably opposed to one another. The struggle was an unequal one, and victory ultimately went to the more stable and prosperous Seljuks, who incorporated the Danishmend lands after a major victory in 1176. The Danishmends and their followers, now evicted, fled to the western marches of Anatolia, where they again took up the frontier fight against the Byzantine Empire. At this moment, Byzantium was also attacked from the West by the Fourth Crusade.

The event of the Fourth Crusade that had by far the greatest consequence was the Latin occupation of Constantinople in 1204 and the resultant dispersion of the Byzantines to several successor states in Anatolia and around the Black Sea. A strong Greek state was established under the dispossessed Byzantine emperor, Theodore Lascaris, with its center at Iznik. Another state was founded around Trebizond by Alexis Comenus. With the Byzantine emperor resident in Anatolia and devoting all his resources to the defense of his realm, the Seljuks of Rum found it difficult to advance against the strong system of fortifications thrown up by the Lascarids to guard the eastern border of their lands. The ghazis found more profitable areas in the north and south. After the ghazi raids came the Seljuk state, taking possession of Sinope on the Black Sea and Antalya on the Mediterranean. For close to half a century the Seljuk-Byzantine frontier remained relatively quiet and free from the raids of the ghazis, a situation favorable to the interests of the rulers on both sides, enabling them to devote their attention to internal problems.

Two momentous events served to break that stalemate on the frontier. One was the Mongol invasion, and the other the reconquest of Constantinople by the Byzantines. On June 2, 1243, a Mongol army defeated the Seljuks near Köse Dagh in eastern Anatolia. The Mongols raided deep into Asia Minor, but they did not do away with the Seljuks of Rum. Instead, they reduced the once proud kingdom to a vassal state, in which condition it lingered until the death of the last subjugated sultan in 1307 or 1308. Weakened by the encounter with the Mongols and by internal factors as well, the Seljuks could no longer restrain the ghazis from attacking on the frontier with Byzantium. At the same time, the older frontier elements were now strengthened by new forces. These included Turcomans, most of whom had been driven out of their old pastures by the Mongols, and peasants fleeing the burdens of taxation, as well as dervishes and other holy men who had led the resistance against the Mongols in Persia. The dislocation of government and society engendered by the Mongol invasion and the subsequent collapse of the Seljuks created in Anatolia a new state of frenzy. New leaders appeared, the most notable being Karaman ibn Musa Sufi. His descendants, the Karamanids, founded a border principality in the foothills of the Taurus Mountains around Ermenik. All along the frontier ghazi warfare against Byzantium resumed.

Resumption of frontier hostilities coincided with the reconquest of Constantinople by the Greeks under Emperor Michael VIII Palaeologus in 1261. Removal of the heart of the empire from Anatolia to Constantinople had immense consequences. Reestablished in Constantinople under the Palaeologi, the Byzantine Empire focused its attention on the Balkans. The defense system erected in Anatolia by the Lascarids was allowed to deteriorate. Ghazi raids soon revealed the weaknesses in those defenses, and the ghazis intensified their drive in the face of crumbling resistance. Many local Greek inhabitants, feeling themselves deserted by the Byzantine forces, threw in their lot with the ghazis, facilitating absorption of western Anatolia. Early in the fourteenth century the Palaeologi were driven from that region. Western Asia Minor was now almost entirely in the hands of the Turks, who were organized into a number of Turkish ghazi emirates, or "principalities." These emirates were the products of borderland warfare and were imbued with the ghazi spirit. The emirs, or chiefs, had led the bands that conquered the various districts, and they became the founders of dynasties of varying fortunes, some of longer duration than others.

THE EMIRATE
OF OSMAN

One of these emirates, the Emirate of Osman, located in the area around Dorylaeum (modern Eskishehir), with Sögüt as its center, was smaller and less powerful than the rest. Despite its comparative insignificance and weakness at the outset, the Emirate of Osman alone achieved lasting fame by forging the borderland principality into the Ottoman Empire. Its rival emirates enjoyed prosperity for a short period of time and then disintegrated under the pressure of internal feuds. What spared the Emirate of Osman from this fate was the fact that it was the ghazi state *par excellence*. Its borders were smack up against the Byzantine defense perimeter that guarded Iznik and Constantinople, and it faced stronger resistance than that met by any other emirate. Locked in this years-long struggle with a great Christian adversary, the emirate's stature rose among its peers, especially after Osman and his ghazis defeated a large Byzantine force at the battle of Baphaeon in 1301.

Osman's fame spread and he attracted to his standard a number of other leaders, or beys, each of whom brought his own followers. These beys, like the other ghazis who joined him, owed loyalty to Osman. As Osman's power grew, that loyalty came more and more to imply Osman's ascendancy over the other beys and their men. His followers took his name and became known as the Ottomans. For those who joined forces with Osman, martyrdom and glory were not the only rewards available; wealth too was to be had, for the Ottoman-held territories straddled the important caravan trade route between Konya and Constantinople.

ORHON With booty and the dictates of strategy uppermost in mind, Osman moved against the leading cities of northwestern Anatolia, blockading Bursa, Iznik, and Nicomedia (modern Izmid). Their capture was left to his son and successor, Orhon (1326–1362). Bursa fell in 1326, Iznik in 1331, and Izmid in 1337. Orhon chose Bursa for his capital, and it remained the Ottoman chief seat until 1402. Bursa is today rich in architectural monuments from that period, including mosques, mosque schools, and sepulchers. In 1336 Orhon took advantage of a succession struggle to absorb the adjacent Emirate of Karasi, thereby extending his territory to the Marmara and Aegean coasts. They now faced the Dardanelles. Beyond lay Europe.

As a ghazi state the Ottoman emirate was geared for conquest. It constantly had to expand, gain new territory, and provide new outlets for the energies of the ghazis. The straits were but a physical barrier, and a narrow one at that, and were soon overcome by the ghazis, who were urged on by psychological, religious, and economic motives. The initial incursion of the Ottomans into Europe was made at the request of the Byzantine Emperor John VI Cantacuzenus, who was engaged in a civil war with the rival house of the Palaeologi. Greek emperors had long been accustomed to hiring Turkish mercenaries as shock troops in their interminable internal feuds. John Cantacuzenus sought the aid of the Ottomans at the recommendation of his usual ally, Umur Bey of Izmir, who was busy fending off a Christian crusading fleet sent to dislodge him from his base. This new relationship between the emperor and the Ottomans was cemented by the marriage of John's daughter Theodora to Orhon. The Ottomans mounted a campaign that carried them as far as Adrianople (modern Edirne) in Thrace. The emperor then attempted to convince his new relations by marriage to remove their warriors from the bridgehead they had established in 1352 at Tzympe on the Gallipoli peninsula.

Once the Ottomans had seen the booty to be had and the possibilities presented by the situation in the Balkans, they were in no mood to listen favorably to requests for self-denial. "Do unto others before others do unto you," appears to have been a sound guiding principle on the frontier. Although the Ottomans were ostensibly auxiliaries of the Greek emperor, they were in fact acting in their own interests in Rumeli ("land of the Byzantines," as they called the Balkans). These Ottoman expeditions were directed by Orhon's eldest son, Suleiman, who was commander of the marches. The frontier against the Christians had now been shifted from Anatolia to Europe.

Early in March 1354 an earthquake wrecked the walls of Gallipoli and several other nearby fortress towns. This natural catastrophe, like some heavenly reward for their ceaseless struggle against the unbelievers, provided the Ottomans with a secure base from which to expand in the Balkans. Suleiman and his warriors occupied and fortified the wrecked towns in the wake of the fleeing, terrified inhabitants. A steady stream of ghazis, mostly men who preferred to take their chances on the frontier rather than remain in overpopulated western Anatolia, but also including some forcibly relocated by the Ottomans, poured from Anatolia into the newly captured regions. The Turks were settling in for a long stay.

Suleiman pressed northward into the Balkans. His accidental death in 1357 did not halt the Ottomans' advance;

Suleiman's younger brother Murad took over as commander of the frontier, assisted by his tutor. It was Ottoman practice until the reign of Mohammed III (1595–1603) to entrust young princes with the responsibility of command, usually as provincial governors. Under the guidance of their tutors, the princes were schooled in the affairs of government, reflecting the Turco-Mongol tradition that government was a family affair.

Murad's warriors took the stronghold of Edirne in 1361. From there the advance was pressed on in three directions: on the left toward Serres and Salonika, on the right toward the Black Sea, and in the center toward Philippopolis and Sofia. Serres fell in 1383, Sofia in 1385, Nish in 1386, and the key port of Salonika in 1387. Behind the advance, immigrants from Anatolia continued to flood in and settle on the conquered lands. In 1365 Murad I (1362–1389), by then ruler in his own right, moved the capital from Bursa to Edirne to expedite the consolidation of Ottoman conquests in the west.

OTTOMAN METHODS OF CONQUEST

The Ottomans' expansion in the Balkans was facilitated by both the internal situation they encountered and their methods of conquest. Geography and politics are closely linked in the Balkans. The mountains are not a significant obstacle to the passage of armies. Control of several riverways gives access to the valley of the Danube. Hungary and Central Europe are vulnerable if the Danube is reached at any point above the Iron Gate. Invaders can easily move into Moldavia and Walachia, and then along the Black Sea coast. Defense of such a vast area demands political unification or, lacking political unification, requires cooperation and coordination. In the last quarter of the fourteenth century the Balkans were not politically unified, and their inhabitants, torn by internal rivalries and mutual jealousies, were incapable of presenting the Ottomans with unified resistance.

The Balkans had gained a semblance of unity in 1350 through the creation of a Serbian empire under Stephen Dushan, who had ascended the throne some two decades earlier. By 1350 Dushan's empire stretched through Albania, Serbia, Macedonia, and Thrace. After his death in 1355, however, the empire quickly disintegrated. In the scramble for realization of private ambitions that ensued after Stephen Dushan's demise, local lords and noble families did not hesitate to ally themselves with the Ottomans. Willing vassals were to be had for the asking.

Ottoman methods of conquest were well suited to just such a situation. There were two distinct phases, or stages, in Ottoman conquest. In the first stage they sought to establish some form of control, usually suzerainty, over adjacent territories in the path of their expansion. These territories were first subdued, some more than once, and then reduced to the status of tributary vassals, who were required to provide troops for the campaigns. The vassals, either indigenous dynasties, nobles, or leading families, preserved their independence and political identities. Shishman of Bulgaria, for a time one of the leading contestants in the competition for dominance in Bulgaria, recognized Murad I as his overlord, and Marko Kraljević, one of the Serbian chieftains, also cooperated with him. Albanian local lords, most of them of foreign origin and caught in the web of competing rivalries, also placed themselves under Ottoman suzerainty.

In the second stage the Ottomans eliminated the local ruling vassals and formally annexed the territories. The establishment of direct control involved the introduction of the timar system into the newly conquered domain. Institution of the timar system entailed a survey of all inhabitants and revenue-producing property units within the new domain. This information was recorded in cadastral registers. Then rights to a share in the income produced through taxation in that domain were granted to the sultan's loyal supporters. Those rights were known as timars, and the man who received such a right was a timariot, or timar-holder. Grants were made usually in return for military service. With few exceptions the timar-holder had to campaign as a mounted and fully armed warrior. He served with the other timar-holders in his area under the command of their bey. Through the timar system the Ottomans created a gentry class that was loyal to the sultan, and in this early period the timariots represented the cream of the Ottoman fighting forces. The timariot leaders were the great beys who surrounded the sultan, campaigned alongside him, and resided at court during periods of peace. At this time most of the high-ranking positions in the state were concentrated in their hands.

Under Murad I both the Ottomans and their vassals were content with the first phase of the Ottoman method of conquest. The vassals benefited by security of possession and status, and the Ottomans were assured of financial gain through the tribute paid by their vassals, loyal supporters on the battlefields, and a secure hinterland behind the expanding frontier. This arrangement was especially useful in the Balkans, where the Serbs, Bosnians, and Bulgarians welcomed Ottoman support against the Hungarians. In Anatolia the Ottomans also had their vassals, but the arrangement presented some particularly complex problems. Islam forbids waging war on coreligionists, so the Ottomans were hard pressed to make their annexations appear in conformity with religious law. Although the Ottomans attempted to placate the Anatolian ghazi chiefs through the distribution to them of lucrative land grants in the Balkans, their actions still elicited severe criticism. Leading the chorus against the Ottomans was their chief rival in Anatolia, the Turcoman house of Karaman.

Having established their center in the old Seljuk capital of Konya, the Karamanids deemed themselves heirs to the Seljuk High Islamic traditions and the sultanate of Rum. The history of Ottoman-Karamanid relations is a long and bloody one, with claims and counterclaims on each side. Essentially, the Karamanids attempted to depict the Ottomans as disloyal to the ghazi tradition by reason of their attacks upon fellow Muslims, and the Ottomans countered with a defense of their position as sultans of the ghazis, whose essential task was carrying on the perennial war against the infidel. They claimed that Karamanid harassment and attack in the rear deflected them from that task. The Ottomans were always careful to secure written religious opinions that sanctioned their campaigns against the Karamanids, who sought to prevent consolidation of their hold on Anatolia.

Difficulties with the Karamanids were indicative of a fundamental problem that plagued the Ottomans even at this early date, and one which they were never able to solve to their full satisfaction. The Ottomans were militarily a two-front state (first as a principality and much more so later as an empire) with but a one-front army. If difficulties arose in Anatolia when they were engaged in military operations in the Balkans, the European campaign would have to be brought to a hasty conclusion in order to shift military resources and the physical presence of the sultan to the east. A similar situation prevailed when the Ottomans were engaged in military operations in the east and trouble arose in the Balkans; the eastern venture would have to be terminated to bring the full weight of the army to the point of danger. Just such a situation developed in 1387 when Murad I was engaged in hostilities with the Karamanids. A revolt broke out in the Balkans, instigated by Serbs who were forced to fight in Murad's armies in Anatolia as a condition of their vassalage. King Lazar of Serbia was joined in this uprising by both Bosnian and Bulgarian contingents. Murad, withdrawing from Anatolia, moved first against Shishman of Bulgaria and then against the Serbs. Victory went to the Ottomans on the plain of Kossovo in 1389 but it was costly. After the fighting, a Serb managed to slay the sultan, bringing a great ghazi career to an end. Murad was immediately succeeded by his son Bajazet (1389–1402). The new ruler inaugurated his reign by taking blood revenge for the assassination of his father. King Lazar, who had fallen captive, was put to death. It was the first lightning stroke in the reign of a man whose electrifying actions had already earned him the sobriquet of the "Thunderbolt."

BAJAZET THE THUNDERBOLT   The fragility of Murad's state in both its Anatolian and Balkan segments, pieced together out of ghazi conquests and vassalage arrangements, was demonstrated by events in the wake of his death. As news of Murad's death spread, the subjugated principalities of Anatolia and the Balkan vassals sought to throw off the Ottoman yoke. Bajazet I used this disloyalty as a justification for moving the pattern of Ottoman conquest into its second stage—the liquidation of his former vassals and the establishment of direct control over their lands. He also sought to bring the more remote Balkan areas, such as Hungary and the Morea, into tributary relationships in preparation for their annexation. He accomplished his objectives through a series of brilliant military campaigns, repeatedly shuttling back and forth between Europe and Asia to carry out his designs against the Muslim emirates and the local rulers in the Balkans, a thunderbolt bent on one objective, the creation of an Ottoman Empire.

Two factors favored Bajazet's attempt at empire building. The first was the internal socioeconomic and religious situation in the Balkans; the second was Bajazet's reliance upon the traditions of High Islam, that served to strengthen centralized government and administration. These two factors were interrelated. Ottoman expansion in the Balkans coincided with a period of deep social unrest there. The Balkan peasantry, subordinated to a ruling aristocracy that knew no limits to its authority, was ground down under the excessive burden of feudal dues heavier and more oppressive than those known to the peasants in Western Europe. In addition to socioeconomic discontent, there was the deep-seated religious animosity between the adherents of the competing Orthodox and Latin Christian churches. The social, economic, and religious problems tended to fuse as the rulers of the Byzantine Empire sought the aid of the West against the Ottomans and held out the possibility of church union in return for such assistance. The peasants, however, remained loyal to the Orthodox church, and, since they were aware of the religious toleration and less-burdensome system of taxation associated with Islam, they preferred Ottoman rule.

The peasants were not the only ones to benefit from the change to direct Ottoman control; the Balkan military aristocracy also gained. The Ottomans were prepared to make room within their own military class for the Christian military aristocracy. Bajazet granted timars to many members of the Balkan military aristocracy on the same basis as those granted to Muslims. He also swept aside the confusing mass of feudal dues previously exacted in services, converting them into manageable cash payments. Many of the former local rulers were now identified with the Ottoman regime, which kept an eye out for abuses in the system and provided the peasants with judicial recourse against overbearing oppression. The peasantry now had a protector in the form of the centralizing Ottoman government, which identified its own interests with the well-being of its subjects. This new attitude was in itself a change with far-reaching effects. The early sultans were solicitous of the welfare of their subjects in other ways, too: They built roads, improved communications, and kept the frontier troops under strict discipline.

By 1394 Bajazet I had reduced Anatolian opposition to Ottoman centralization to two main centers, Konya and Sivas. Europe now panicked at Bajazet's rumored intention to feed his horse at the altar of St. Peter in Rome. Such an ambitious scheme required the consolidation of Ottoman control over the Balkans and the transformation of southeastern Europe into an armed Ottoman camp. Bajazet I sought to subdue the Balkans through attacks spearheaded by the ghazis, now partly transformed into irregular army forces employed as raiders and shock troops, and through campaigns waged by the regular army, composed mostly of feudal cavalry (the timariots) personally commanded in the field by the sultan. By sharing the hardships of the campaign, the sultan preserved his image as the great ghazi leader who constantly expanded the Abode of Islam by conquering lands in the Abode of War.

Bajazet, seeking to take the imperial city situated at the point where he hoped the two halves of his developing empire would meet, commenced his blockade of Constantinople in the spring of 1394. That great and demanding venture did not prevent him, however, from continuing his interests in other areas of the Balkans. In 1395 he personally led an invasion of Hungary, placed his own candidate on the throne of Walachia at the expense of an Hungarian vassal, and rang down the curtain on the checkered career of his disloyal vassal Shishman by having him arrested and executed. Europe could no longer ignore Bajazet's audacity and the threat he posed, and the first joint European effort to save Constantinople was organized, primarily by Sigismund of Hungary, the Pope, and the Duke of Burgundy. Sigismund was the one most clearly threatened because the Ottoman subjugation of Serbia and Bulgaria had opened a path to the Danube. Hungarian interests were also at stake in Walachia and along the Adriatic coast. France was again imbued with crusading zeal and chivalrous ideals. Venice, playing both sides in an effort to protect her commercial interests and her grain supply without enraging the sultan, contributed only her navy to help supply the beleaguered city. The crusading army gathered at Buda and descended the Danube, arriving at Nicopolis. Bajazet, who had returned to the vicinity of Constantinople, swiftly moved to engage the crusaders at Nicopolis. The flower of European knighthood was cut down within three hours on September 25, 1396. Although there would be other ventures, the battle at Nicopolis in effect ended the last real crusade.

Bajazet's victory allowed him to turn his attention once again to Anatolia, where the Karamanids had taken advantage of his preoccupation in the Balkans in order to extend their territories. Victory was again Bajazet's as he took Konya in 1397 and the Sivas area in 1398. Bajazet's authority now extended over most of the area formerly controlled by the Byzantine Empire in the Balkans and Anatolia, except Constantinople, which he now set about to conquer.

Bajazet's blockade of the imperial city might conceivably have resulted in its capitulation had the sultan been able to press on with the siege undisturbed; that, however, was not to be the case. The city's deliverer came not from the West, but from the East. He was the Turco-Mongol conqueror Timur Lenk, known to the West as Tamerlane.

Timur Lenk (Timur the lame), one of the great world conquerors, was born in 1336 of humble Turkish, Muslim origins, in Transoxania. A fierce warrior, he fashioned an empire in Central Asia out of the Mongol successor states and married a descendant of Genghis Khan, thereby uniting

Turkish and Mongol traditions of state. Moving westward, Timur struck against Persia in 1380 and subjugated the Iranian plateau by 1387, making himself a neighbor of the Ottomans. He invaded Anatolia for the first time in 1394 and then reappeared in 1399, claiming suzerainty over Anatolia as the heir of the Mongols. Bajazet countered this pretension with one of his own. In 1394 he had sought and received recognition of his claim to the title of Sultan of Rum. He obtained that recognition from the caliph, the highest political and religious leader of the Muslim world, who had been living at the court of the Mamluk sultan in Cairo since the capture of Baghdad by the Mongols in 1256. Bajazet was no longer a frontier warrior and head of a frontier principality, but the ruler of a great Islamic state.

Timur was somewhat hesitant to attack the man whose reputation as a ghazi had been enhanced by his victory at Nicopolis. War was urged upon him, however, by the Anatolian emirs who had been dispossessed by Bajazet and had taken refuge at Timur's court. They hoped for reinstatement in their domains. Two such imposing figures as Timur and Bajazet could not glower at each other for long without a clash, and it finally took place near Ankara on June 28, 1402. The Ottomans were defeated; Bajazet was taken captive and died in March 1403, a suicide, it is said, while in Timur's hands. The Ottoman state Bajazet had labored so arduously to put together collapsed.

BAJAZET'S
LEGACY

Bajazet's efforts to establish an empire failed. He did, however, leave behind an important legacy that permanently affected Ottoman government, society, and administration. Bajazet I was responsible for the introduction of centralized government, with its fiscal techniques and the timar system. He also greatly developed the slave system. In imitation of the Anatolian Seljuks even the earliest Ottoman rulers had trained young slaves of non-Muslim origins, called *ghulams*, for palace and state service. In frontier warfare there was no shortage of slaves, and Murad I is generally credited with organizing the first of the janissary units from prisoners of war that came to him as the one-fifth share of the booty allowed the sultan by religious law. *Ghulams* trained during Bajazet's reign were given important military and administrative positions, and some were even assigned timars, mostly in Anatolia, where they replaced the indigenous Muslim aristocracy of the various emirates absorbed by the Ottomans. Bajazet's slaves, known as the slaves of the Porte, further strengthened central authority by giving him a military force and administrative officers totally dependent upon his own will through which to exercise his authority. He also strengthened the religious establishment, attracting Muslim scholars, teachers, and judges from the neighboring, older Islamic states, especially from Egypt, as he sought to transform his domains into a traditional Islamic monarchy and himself into a great Muslim monarch.

Anything that increased the power of the central authority was in effect a blow to the position of the ghazis and their leaders. Resentment on the part of the ghazis against Bajazet's innovations in government and religion and against his grants of timars to Christians and slaves is amply reflected in the early Ottoman chronicles, and it played an important role in Bajazet I's failure to realize his imperial ambitions. He was unable to fuse the diverse elements of his state into a coherent whole before Timur put an end to his career. It remained for others of the Ottoman dynasty to replace totally the power of the frontier lords with the authority of the central government and to establish an empire. Nevertheless, his achievements were influential in the process of putting the state back together again after the damage wrought by Tamerlane.

RECOVERY AND
RENEWED
CONQUEST

The decade following the defeat at Ankara is referred to by Turkish historians as the Interregnum. Like most such periods in other histories, it was a "time of troubles" for the Ottomans, too. Timur did not disappoint the Anatolian emirs. He reinstated them in their possessions and reduced the Ottoman lands in Anatolia to what they had been on Bajazet I's accession. Bajazet's son Musa accompanied his father into captivity. Three other sons recognized Timur's suzerainty and were installed as local rulers: Suleiman in

Edirne, Mohammed in Amasya, and Isa in Bursa. When Timur died in 1405, the Ottoman princes entered into an internecine struggle for sole possession of the right to direct the Ottoman future. Mohammed won in 1413, assisted by the subjects who favored the reunification of the Ottoman domains under a single sultan with a strong central government. Primarily these elements were the timar-holders, who realized that only a government that succeeded in restoring order and union could enforce their legal claims to their holdings, and the slaves of the Porte, whose positions were dependent solely upon the sultan.

Circumspection characterized Mohammed I's reign (1413–1421) once he succeeded in gaining sole rule. As long as the power of Timur's son Shahrukh loomed in the background, Mohammed could not move militarily against the restored Anatolian emirates. He also had to deal gently with Constantinople because of the Ottoman pretenders to the throne who sought Byzantine support. Harassed by internal revolts, pretenders, and organizational problems, Mohammed had to be careful not to arouse any general European reaction that might block his attempts at restoration. Thus his short but crucial reign was a holding operation that succeeded in preventing total disintegration of the Ottoman domains.

Recovery began in earnest under Mohammed's son Murad II (1421–1451). The new sultan secured his throne by defeating his uncle, the pretender known as the False Mustafa, in the Balkans. (Ottoman pretenders have much in common with counterparts in Russia, such as the False Dimitri who appeared on the scene at the beginning of the seventeenth century.) Murad II then crossed over to Anatolia to deal with those who had seized Ottoman lands while he was away. Murad reincorporated the emirates of Western Anatolia but stopped short of the Karamanid domains in central Anatolia, over which Shahrukh claimed suzerainty on the grounds that they had been part of the territory subject to the Ilkhanids. In Europe, the holy war that had played such an instrumental role in the early expansion was resuming on two fronts, against Venice and Hungary. Venice was committed to a policy of maintaining and expanding her trading empire in the East. Her purchase of Salonika from the Palaeologi in 1423 precipitated the conflict with Murad, who sought to reestablish Turkish control over that important port lost to the Byzantines in 1402. The Ottomans succeeded in occupying Salonika in 1430, and a peace settlement was arranged with Venice.

Murad was now free to devote his efforts to expansion in the direction of Hungary, as many ghazis were urging. King Sigismund's death in December 1437 opened the door to Ottoman attack. Murad marched into Serbia in 1438 and seized the rich silver mines and the key fortress of Semendria. In 1440 Murad besieged Belgrade, the most important fortress protecting southern Hungary from Turkish raids, but after six months he was forced to withdraw. Ottoman raiders then sought to invest Transylvania, but their efforts were totally rebuffed by one of the truly remarkable figures of the age, János Hunyadi, governor of Transylvania.

Hunyadi's heroic efforts evoked a response in Europe, and talk of crusade was again in the air. Without waiting for assistance from the West, Hunyadi launched a campaign against the Ottomans in which he took Nish and Sofia in 1443. Because Murad was again faced with trouble in Anatolia—this time from the Karamanids—and had lost many of his top commanders in battle against Hunyadi, he sought a peaceful settlement, which was reached in June 1444. He then crossed over to Anatolia and arranged a settlement with the Karamanids as well.

Murad is said to have been a contemplative man who did not like war. He had grown weary of constant campaigning, and, with his European and Anatolian frontiers stabilized by peace treaties, Murad decided to abdicate in favor of his twelve-year-old son, Mohammed, who was to be tutored by influential men of state. One was the vizier Chandarli Halil Pasha, scion of a famous house that had served the sultans for generations; the other was Husrev Molla, a prominent figure in the religious establishment. Murad then went to the region of Bursa in hopes of enjoying a peaceful retirement spent in pious meditation.

Murad's hopes were soon disappointed. Plans had been

underway in the West for a large-scale campaign against the Ottomans. The retirement of Murad encouraged a false belief that this action spelled Ottoman military weakness, and great hopes of support from the local population spurred on the planners. Meanwhile the Ottoman commanders, especially Halil Pasha, implored Murad to return and take command of the army, fearing to leave the fate of the state in the hands of a child. Murad responded to the call and led his army to a crushing victory at Varna in November 1444. Murad retired once again to Bursa, only to be recalled to the throne when the janissaries in Edirne rose in rebellion. He remained on the throne from 1446 until his death in 1451. During those years he inflicted a severe defeat upon Hunyadi in 1448 and directed Ottoman raids into Albania, Greece, and Serbia. The recovery of Ottoman domains that had been initiated at the start of Murad's reign had gone well, and at the time of his death only Constantinople remained, a ripe plum waiting to be picked. Europe, however, did not fear for the safety of the capital city, seeing the reenthroned sultan Mohammed II as weak, young, and ineffective. This was a typical Western misconception about the Turks. Mohammed II, only nineteen when he came to the throne, stood at the threshold of a great career of conquest that would inscribe his name in Ottoman annals as "the Conqueror."

MOHAMMED THE CONQUEROR

Mohammed II may have been young, but he was not politically inexperienced, nor did he lack for sage and energetic counselors. He had been gaining experience in governmental affairs since about the age of eleven, when he had been sent out from Edirne to be governor of Manisa in Anatolia. The key to an understanding of Mohammed's career and to much of subsequent Ottoman history as well must be sought in the events concerned with his first, short reign, and the concepts he carried away from that experience.

Two people had the most to do with shaping Mohammed's ideas. These were Chandarli Halil Pasha and Zaganos Pasha. Halil represented the traditions of High Islam and came from the ulema, the learned religious establishment. He stood for a policy of peace that would allow for internal consolidation. Zaganos was a slave, one of the slaves of the Porte, and had been Mohammed's tutor in Manisa. He advocated a policy of expansion within the framework of the ghazi tradition and consistently urged the capture of Constantinople, in opposition to Halil's conciliatory views. Halil Pasha, using the janissaries as the instrument of his policy, implored Murad first to assume leadership of the army and then to return to the throne. He is suspected of having incited the janissary revolt in Edirne that resulted in the conclusion of Mohammed's first reign and in his father's return to power. This maneuver naturally left an impression on young Mohammed. He formed his policy, bided his time, and planned his revenge. It is an interesting characteristic of the Ottomans, and even of modern-day Turkish society, that accounts are kept of inflicted wrongs, and at the proper moment these accounts are settled to the applause of the onlookers. Halil Pasha's days were numbered.

Mohammed's policy, conceived during the turmoil of his unhappy early experiences, had four essential points. He must rid himself of Chandarli Halil Pasha, reorganize the janissaries to eliminate any divisive elements and make them more dependent upon himself, take Constantinople, and make the holy war again the guiding principle of the state. The conquest of Constantinople was the crucial point. He could not acquire the loyalty and support necessary to move against Halil without first achieving a significant military victory. Once he had taken Constantinople even the janissaries would be powerless to resist a move directed against themselves. The issue was plain, and the sides were drawn. Zaganos urged the conquest of Constantinople; Halil, ever fearful of a crusade, counseled withdrawal.

Constantinople had not surrendered and therefore was considered legitimate booty under Muslim religious law. The promise of booty encouraged the troops to press the attack on to victory. The city fell on May 29, 1453. The day after the conquest Chandarli Halil Pasha was arrested and ultimately executed. A debt had been repaid. But the dismissal and execution of Halil was more meaningful than just the fulfillment of a personal vendetta: it signified an end to the share in state power formerly enjoyed by the old, established Muslim families. With the exception of his last chief minister, Mohammed II selected all his grand viziers from his personal slaves, thus concentrating power in his own hands.

With Halil Pasha out of the way, Mohammed II reorganized and expanded the janissary corps. He turned the new janissary units into a well-paid, excellently equipped standing force loyal only to him. He stationed his janissaries in provincial garrisons, where they served to represent the central authority and in effect destroyed the last remnants of independent authority enjoyed by the beys of the frontier. With such a powerful force at his constant beck and call, Mohammed was stronger than any possible internal foe. With much the same attitude that characterized the Tudors' destruction of their overmighty subjects, Mohammed II rendered himself supreme over both the frontier lords and the aristocratic Muslim families.

Once Mohammed II had established himself as the absolute sovereign, the sole wielder of power and authority, he turned his energies to the realization of his fourth point, renewal of the holy war. Through the holy war the Conqueror consolidated and extended his empire. Again, advances in Europe alternated with drives into Anatolia. Athens fell in 1458; Serbia in 1459; and Morea in 1460. Bosnia was absorbed in 1464, and the Bosnian nobility, most of whom converted to Islam, joined in raids against Hungary and in the defense of the frontier. At the conclusion of the long war with Venice (1463–1479) the Ottoman's controlled Negropont and the Adriatic coastline. This policy of eliminating the relics of Byzantine sovereignty sealed the doom of the Palaeologi-related despotates of the Morea and of the Greek Empire of Trebizond.

The conquest of Trebizond was part of a successful plan to dominate the Black Sea coastline of Anatolia and to convert the Black Sea into an Ottoman lake. That plan involved the elimination also of the Genoese trading bases along the Black Sea coast, especially their main emporium of Kefe in the Crimea. Finally the entire Crimea was brought under Ottoman suzerainty when the khan of the Golden Horde accepted status as an Ottoman vassal in 1475. Thus a vast trading area, linking Anatolia with routes north into Russia and Central Asia and west into Europe, came into Ottoman hands.

Mohammed conducted a successful campaign against the Karamanids which resulted in the annexation of their lands in central Anatolia in 1468. After 1468 members of the Karamanid dynasty carried on the struggle in the Taurus Mountains aided by the Turcoman leader Uzun Hasan. Venice and the Papacy attempted to enter into an effective alliance with Hasan in an effort to open a second front against the Ottomans. This recurrent European dream of accomplishing the ruin of the Ottomans by compelling them to fight in both Europe and Anatolia at the same time came to naught when the Ottomans defeated Uzun Hasan in 1473, but the policy would surface time and time again whenever a strong party appeared at the Ottoman rear. With the incorporation of the Karamanids, only the Zulkadir Turcomans for a short time and the Mamluks of Egypt for a somewhat longer period remained to dispute Ottoman domination of southeastern Anatolia.

ISTANBUL Despite Mohammed II's almost incessant involvement in warfare during the thirty years of his reign, he still found time to attend to the transformation of Constantinople, now called Istanbul, into a city worthy of being the capital of the Islamic empire. He repopulated the city, by both encouraging and forcing the immigration of people with the skills needed in an urban environment. The city walls were repaired, and Kritovoulos, the Greek chronicler of Mohammed's reign, tells us that the sultan ordered his wealthy and able people to build homes and beautiful public buildings, baths, inns, marketplaces, workshops, and mosques. Mohammed provided the example by ordering the construction of the great mosque that bears his name and its auxiliary institutions: lodgings for travelers, a hospital, an almshouse, and a college for instruction in the Islamic sciences, law, and medicine. These and similar edifices in the capital and elsewhere in the empire were financed through the wakf ("pious foundation"), an Islamic institution whereby revenues from income-producing properties were assigned in perpetuity in order to provide for certain public services. Population statistics show Mohammed's success in infusing new life into the city. Prior to the conquest it is estimated that the number of its inhabitants had fallen to about 30,000. A census dated 1478, however, indicates that the population had risen to close to 100,000; and by the end of the sixteenth century, it is placed at 700,000, making Istanbul by far the most populous city of Europe. The city's growth was a fitting tribute to the task of rebuilding commenced by Mohammed the Conqueror and celebrated in verse by the seventeenth-century Ottoman poet Nabi.

We have not seen its peer in any land
It has none, save perhaps in Paradise.

The threshold of the Ottoman Sultanate
The delight of the imperial realm . . .

There is no land or city that is like it
No place to live that can compare with it.*

The beautification of Istanbul and the waging of ceaseless warfare were not accomplished without strain, especially in the economic and political realms. Because of this strain Mohammed was forced to undertake a number of unpopular measures. Several times he issued new coins, withdrawing the old ones at only five-sixths of their value. He instituted provincial monopolies on such staples as salt, candle wax, and soap. He let these monopolies to private individuals for the benefit of the treasury and to the detriment of the people, who had to pay higher prices. The

---

*Quoted in Bernard Lewis, *Istanbul and the Civilization of the Ottoman Empire* (Norman, Okla.: University of Oklahoma Press, 1963), pp. 98–100. Copyright © 1963 by the University of Oklahoma Press.

policy that provoked the greatest resentment, however, centered around the confiscation of property consecrated as pious foundations. The sultan's view was that since the land had originally belonged to him, it had been turned into private domains and made wakf through irregularities. He repossessed these lands in order to grant them again as fiefs to timar-holders, thus increasing the size of his military potential. His strategy aroused much opposition, since wealthy and influential families had converted their properties into family wakfs in order to safeguard their positions. The superintendent of such a family foundation, who usually received for his services a handsome stated income from the endowment, was himself a member of the family.

BAJAZET II   Mohammed had been able to keep in check the discontent that was aroused by these policies, but it broke out upon his death in 1481. That discontent was the basis of a struggle for the throne between his two sons, Cem (born 1459) and Bajazet (born 1447 or 1448). At the time of his father's death Cem was governor of the Karamanid territories, with his provincial seat at Konya. Bajazet was governor of Amasya. Cem, who favored his father's measures, had the support of the grand vizier, and Bajazet had the support of all those who had opposed the economic and political policies of his father, especially the janissaries. After a number of battles and campaigns, Bajazet's superior forces defeated Cem, who took refuge in 1482 with the Knights of St. John on the island of Rhodes. They sent him to France, and he became a pawn in the game of international politics. Cem's presence meant prestige and income for whichever country harbored him, since the sultan would pay handsomely to keep him in captivity and out of the Ottoman lands. In 1489 Cem was transferred to the custody of the Pope, and he died in Naples in February 1495.

The character of Bajazet II's reign was largely determined by the measures he was compelled to undertake in order to assure the security of his throne and the safety of his empire. At the very outset, in order to rally janissary support against his brother Cem, he was forced to abandon two of his father's policies, the frequent issuance of new coinage and the seizure of wakf properties. He also agreed to restore previously confiscated properties. As long as Cem was alive Bajazet feared the possibility of an invasion by Christian powers using Cem as a political weapon. That fear prevented Bajazet from committing his resources to the limit in any single military venture either in Europe or in the East. This in part accounts for the several military stalemates between the Ottomans and the Mamluks, who had embraced Cem's cause. What success the Ottomans had along the frontier with Hungary was mainly the work of the ghazis. Poland began to figure prominently in Ottoman concerns when the Poles sought to break through the Ottoman and Crimean Tartar barrier that blocked their access to the Black Sea. Ghazis and Tartar horsemen raided deep into Podolia and Galicia in 1498. The Tartars were to loom large during the next two centuries in the history of the Black Sea steppe, a region that provided thousands upon thousands of captives for the Ottoman slave markets.

Three significant developments occurred in Bajazet II's reign that played important roles in determining much of the subsequent course of Ottoman history. One of these developments was the growth in the size and strength of the Ottoman navy. This growth had important implications for extension of the holy war and ghazi warfare to challenge Venice and Spain in the Adriatic, Aegean, and Mediterranean seas. With a viable naval force to balance their feared army, the Ottomans became part of the European diplomatic system, an ally much sought after by those who wished to prevent the domination of Europe by a universal monarchy. The second development was the rise of the Safavid house in Persia, yet another threat to Ottoman supremacy in the east. The Safavid ruler, Shah Ismail, had converted a Sufi order founded by his ancestor in the fourteenth century into a militant, expanding Shi'ite state. Shi'ism, a major division of the Islamic religion, originated in the split in the Islamic community that developed upon the death of Muhammad. The Shi'ites supported the claim of Ali, Muhammad's son-in-law, to the caliphate, and the

Sunnites, who included the Ottomans, accepted the caliphate of Abu Bakr, Muhammad's actual successor. That split perpetuated itself in Islam, and the Sunnite and Shi'ite communities were mutually antagonistic. The Shi'ite Safavids were conducting a vigorous propaganda campaign among the Turcoman tribes of eastern Anatolia. Ottoman administrative and fiscal policies had alienated the Turcomans; and Shi'ite ideas, tinged with anarchical radical and social overtones, spread among them. Bajazet sought to diminish the threat of losing large areas of Asia Minor to the Safavids by deporting suspected Shi'ite elements to the newly conquered lands in the Morea. A serious Shi'ite revolt in Asia Minor in 1511 revealed the ineffectiveness of this policy. The third development, which future research may well show to have had the greatest consequences, was the circumnavigation of Africa by Vasco da Gama in 1498. One of its consequences may have been to influence Selim I's drive to conquer the Mamluk domains in Egypt.

Bajazet himself did not have to deal with the effects of these developments. By 1511 it was evident that the aging sultan, who was closer in character to his contemplative grandfather, Murad II, than to his energetic father, Mohammed II, was losing his grip on the state. Although Mohammed II is said to have raised to the status of a law (*kanun*) the practice whereby upon his accession a sultan murdered his brothers together with his brothers' male offspring in an effort to prevent wars of succession, civil strife still threatened. Until 1617, when the rule was adopted that the oldest surviving male member of the dynasty succeeded to the throne, there was no "law" of succession. Princes sought to outmaneuver their brothers, if there were any, in quest of the sultanate. Bajazet II had won out over Cem, and now his sons Ahmed and Selim were preparing for conflict. Ahmed was the governor of Amasya, which was closer to Istanbul than Selim's provincial seat of Trebizond. Success usually crowned the efforts of the son who managed to arrive at Istanbul first, secure control of the treasury and state archives, and win over the janissaries. Selim, aware of his geographical disadvantage, forced his father to grant him a governorship in the Balkans, and then with the support of the janissaries he marched upon Istanbul and compelled his father to abdicate in his favor in April 1512.

SELIM
THE GRIM

Selim I (1512–1520), a man whose determination and ferocity won for him the sobriquet "the Grim," had first to render his throne secure before he could launch upon any military ventures. This he did by ordering the death of his nephews and having his older brother done away with. Another brother risked all in an open battle with Selim's forces, but he was captured and killed during the rout of his army.

The way was now clear for the expected confrontation with Shah Ismail. Culturally the Ottomans, like the Seljuks before them, were deeply indebted to Persian traditions in the fields of literature, art, government, law, and scholarship. Many office holders throughout the Ottoman Empire had migrated to the Ottoman lands from points further east. One can speak meaningfully of a shared Turco-Persian culture stretching from India to the Danube. Despite the elements that bound the Ottomans and Safavids together, their differences, both religious and political, were even greater. The Ottomans could not tolerate an expansion-minded state of any religious stripe on their eastern frontier without instilling in the upstart a sense of fear and respect. The Safavids, inheritors of the Timurid tradition of hegemony in central Anatolia and the ancient Iranian view of divine kingship, were galvanized into action by their heretical beliefs. They were unperturbed by the prospects of a clash. Venice, reviving the second-front scheme, evinced an interest in the shah's situation.

Preparatory to the campaign against Shah Ismail, Selim hunted down suspected Shi'ite supporters in eastern Anatolia, and it is said that some 40,000 were killed. After a long march from Istanbul, made more arduous by the scorched-earth policy of the Safavids in their own territory, Selim forced Ismail to give battle at Chaldiran, northeast of Lake Van, on April 23, 1514. Ottoman artillery carried the day. The Safavids fled, and Selim entered Tabriz on September 5. Selim wished to follow up his victory in the next campaigning season by wintering in Tabriz, but the janissaries, tired and weary, forced him to abandon those plans.

Selim I also had to deal with the Mamluks. In the course of swift campaigns in 1516 and 1517, during which Ottoman artillery and firepower overcame Mamluk horsemanship, he had made himself master of the Mamluk domains, including Syria, Egypt, and the Hejaz. Selim's drive to the Red Sea may have been his response to the oceanic revolution ushered in by Vasco da Gama's circumnavigation of Africa and by the extension of Portuguese naval strength to the Indian Ocean. Ottoman expansion into North Africa between 1515 and 1519 can be seen in the same light. The Mamluks, hampered by a lack of timber and possessed of a cultural tradition that extolled horsemanship and knightly virtues to the detriment of firearms and naval skills, had not been equal to the task of defending Islamic interests against the Portuguese. By taking over the Mamluk domains, the Ottomans had inherited the role of defender of the holiest places in Islam, the cities of Mecca and Medina, which were the cradle of Islam. The Ottoman sultan was now the supreme Islamic ruler and as such had to shoulder responsibility for resisting the invaders. By 1517 Selim was already too late to check Portuguese expansion in the Indian Ocean, but until the mid-sixteenth century he carried the battle to the Portuguese by constructing fleets at Suez using Cilician timber and artisans who had gained experience in the dockyards of Istanbul, and employing commanders battle-tested in the Mediterranean. Although Ottoman attempts to expel the Christian intruders were unsuccessful, the Portuguese never fully dominated the Indian Ocean trade, and spices continued to appear in markets of the eastern Mediterranean.

During the eight years of Selim I's reign Christendom knew a period of comparative peace, free of any large-scale imperial campaigns in Europe. His death in 1520 and the accession of his son Suleiman marked the end of that respite. Under the leadership of this dynamic young sultan, Ottoman military power once again swung westward and the traditional *ghaza* policy was resumed.

At this time the predominant power in Christian Europe was Charles V of the house of Hapsburg. Contesting for the prize of universal monarchy was Francis I, of the house of Valois. With this dominant theme of Hapsburg-Valois rivalry influencing his policies, Suleiman set about to gain two objectives that had eluded his predecessors. The first of these objectives was Belgrade; the second the island of Rhodes.

Belgrade was the gateway to Hungary and Central Europe; Rhodes was the stepping stone to the establishment of Ottoman supremacy in the Mediterranean Sea. Belgrade fell to Suleiman on August 29, 1521, and on Christmas Day of the following year he made his triumphal entry into the citadel of Rhodes, which the Knights of St. John were forced to abandon after a long and terrible siege. Suleiman had succeeded where even Mohammed the Conqueror had failed.

Like that illustrious ancestor, Suleiman was a relentless campaigner. His reign witnessed the extension of Ottoman dominion in Europe, Persia, the Mediterranean, and Arabia. The Ottomans became locked in an unyielding struggle with the Hapsburgs that had all the overtones of a contest for world supremacy. After 1525, following Francis I's defeat at the hands of the Hapsburgs at Pavia, the French sought Ottoman support as a counterweight to Hapsburg power. The French-Ottoman alliance became an integral part of the European state system and a factor in the balance of power. Although at times France proved to be an unreliable ally, the Ottomans pressed forward on their own western flank, where their advance became a significant factor in the recognition and spread of Protestantism. Support for France and the Protestants, as well as for other anti-Hapsburg elements, such as the Muslims and Jews ejected from Spain, was the cornerstone of Ottoman policy in Europe at this time.

This anti-Hapsburg posture of the Ottomans is also discernible in the Mediterranean, where the holy war was also waged. The Ottoman ghazi spirit, harnessed to the state policy of alliance with France, found a significant

34

outlet against the Hapsburgs in North Africa and the eastern Mediterranean. The Ottoman admiral Khair ed-Din Barbarossa established control over Algeria and contended with Charles V for Tunis. At Preveza in Greece in 1538 his fleet inflicted a severe defeat upon the Venetians, who were another powerful factor in Mediterranean affairs. Ottoman naval supremacy in the eastern Mediterranean, ushered in by Preveza, endured until the battle of Lepanto in 1571.

Victorious on land and sea, Suleiman was the greatest Islamic ruler of his time. Possession of the holy cities of Mecca and Medina enhanced his status but also carried with it a number of heavy responsibilities. Chief among these was maintenance of security on the pilgrimage routes. This task involved the Ottomans in serious conflict with the Portuguese in the Indian Ocean and with the Muscovites in the Volga basin. The economics of the spice and silk trades and of the northern trade were bound up with the military efforts of the Ottomans to assist their coreligionists in the east and in Central Asia. In addition to defending the Islamic world against its Christian enemies, the Ottomans also had to contend with the Persian Safavids, who were always ready to attack the Ottoman rear.

The European hope of a second front against the Ottomans was rekindled by Charles V, who sought to move the Safavids into action against the Ottomans. Suleiman could not afford to neglect the serious challenge and threat posed by the Safavids. The emergence of any power on their eastern flank, regardless of sectarian considerations, made the Ottomans uneasy. Suleiman mounted two full-scale campaigns against the Safavids, one in 1533 and the other in 1548. Both were preceded by peace or truce arrangements patched together in Europe that enabled the sultan to shift his forces eastward. In the first campaign Suleiman brought Tabriz and Baghdad under his control, along with the important trade routes that passed through those cities. As soon as he turned his attention to Europe, the Safavids retook Tabriz. In the second campaign Suleiman retook Tabriz. The Ottomans were finding it extremely difficult to maintain direct control over such distant areas as Tabriz. Geography, technology, and military organization set the limits to Ottoman expansion in the east, as these factors had in Europe when they failed to take Vienna. Explicitly or implicitly, this fact was recognized in the treaty of Amasya (May 29, 1555) that returned Tabriz to Safavid control and served to set the eastern boundary of the empire for close to a quarter of a century.

With the eastern border stabilized, Suleiman returned to the struggle in the west. The Mediterranean and North Africa became areas of almost constant warfare. In 1565 the Ottomans embarked upon a costly and eventually futile effort to conquer the island of Malta. The next year Suleiman decided to campaign in Hungary. He was over seventy years of age and could sit his horse only with difficulty. Knowing that the Ottoman troops fought better when their sultan was in the field with them, Suleiman set out from Istanbul on his thirteenth campaign at the head of some 200,000 men on May 1, 1566. It proved to be his last campaign. On the night of September 5 he died in his tent, while the siege of Szigetvár was still in progress. His death was kept a secret until his son Selim could assume the throne in Istanbul without turbulence. The poet Baki, friend of the sultan and recipient of his beneficence, expressed in an elegy the melancholy sense of loss he and his fellow Ottomans experienced after having awaited the sultan's return to the capital:

Will not the King awake from sleep? broke has the dawn of day.
Will not he move forth from his tent bright as heaven's display?
Long have our eyes dwelt on the road, and yet no news is come
From yonder land, the threshold of his majesty's array.
The color of his cheek has palled, dry-lipped he lies there,
Even as the rose that from the water sweet is fallen away. . . .
Praise be to God, for He in either World has blessed thee
And writ before your honored name both Martyr and Ghazi.*

---

*Quoted in *A History of Ottoman Poetry*, E. J. W. Gibb (ed.) (London: Luzac and Company, 1904), III, 154.

Chapter 2

Ottoman Society and Institutions

The Ottomans did not realize at once that they had lost more than just a great ghazi with the death of Suleiman the Magnificent. Under his son and successor, Selim II, military pressure against the West was maintained on land and even increased on the Mediterranean. The holy war was extended into new areas, and North Africa became a major zone of confrontation between the Ottomans and the Hapsburgs. By the end of the century, however, some observant foreign ambassadors to Constantinople and some astute Ottoman men of letters would concur that somehow the empire's golden age had come to an end. Keenly aware of the Ottoman fall from grandeur, they would lay the blame upon the corruption of the empire's classic institutions that had flowered in Suleiman's reign. A consideration of those institutions and of Ottoman society is required for a fuller understanding of the development from a frontier ghazi principality into an Islamic empire and of later developments as well.

By the death of Suleiman the Ottoman Empire covered the area now occupied on the map by all or parts of Hungary, Yugoslavia, Albania, Greece, Bulgaria, Rumania, the Ukraine, the Crimea, Turkey, Iran, Iraq, Syria, Lebanon, Jordan, Israel, Saudi Arabia, Yemen, Egypt, Libya,

Tunisia, Algeria, and other lands as well. Population estimates for that period are notoriously unreliable, but a "guesstimate" of some twenty to thirty million people appears reasonable. Superimposed over that broad geographical expanse and congeries of people were a system of government and a social structure that drew inspiration from three major sources: the steppe traditions of Central Asia, the ghazi ideal, and the traditions of High Islam as influenced by Persian practices.

STEPPE, GHAZI, AND CLASS

The steppe tradition contributed principally the notion that sovereignty was the prerogative of a single family chosen by God to bear the burden of rule. As Turkish tribal leaders established dynasties, first in the outer reaches of the Abode of Islam, and then in the Islamic heartland itself, sultans came to exercise the temporal authority that was previously the preserve of the caliphs. The concept of sovereignty as a family possession supplanted the Islamic principle of elective leadership that had already become more honored in the breach than in practice. Among the Ottomans the descendants of Osman ruled in unbroken succession (except during the Interregnum following the battle of Ankara in 1402) until 1923, when Mustafa Kemal Atatürk put an end to the empire and created the modern state of Turkey. In a very real sense then, the Ottoman state and the Ottoman dynasty were inseparable until the twentieth century.

The Ottoman sultans, secure in their hereditary right to rule, both fostered and were themselves impelled by the ghazi urge to conquer the infidel lands for Islam. The Ottoman state owed its existence as well as its continued prosperity and power to conquest. It was a state committed to and organized for conquest. The conquered areas were administered largely in accordance with the social, religious, and political practices and the fiscal procedures of earlier Islamic states. Those practices and procedures were the distillation of Greek ideas, Sassanid Persian views on statecraft, and Islamic legal precepts. Through the Ottoman genius for government and administration, those varied elements, along with several significant innovations,

38

were blended into a new dispensation with its own distinctive stamp and flavor.

Early Islamic society had been characterized by a kind of social equalitarianism, but that trait had quickly disappeared. By the thirteenth century Muslim theoreticians on ethical, social, and political questions had elaborated a view of society that postulated the existence of four social classes and equated each class with a natural element. Nasireddin Tusi (d. 1273) described the classes:

First come the Men of the Pen such as the masters of the sciences and the branches of knowledge, the canon-lawyers, the judges, secretaries, accountants, geometers, astronomers, physicians, and poets, on whose existence depends the order of this world and the next; among the natural elements these correspond to Water. Secondly, the Men of the Sword; fighters, warriors, volunteers, skirmishers, frontier-guardians, sentries, valiant men, supporters of the realm and guardians of the state, by whose intermediacy the world's organization is effected; among the natural elements these correspond to Fire. Thirdly, the Men of Negotiation, merchants who carry goods from one region to another, tradesmen, masters of crafts, and tax-collectors, without whose co-operation the daily life of the species would be impossible; among the natural elements, they are like Air. Fourthly, the Men of Husbandry, such as sowers, farmers, ploughmen, and agriculturalists, who organize the feeding of all the communities, and without whose help the survival of individuals would be out of the question; among the natural elements they have the same rank as Earth.*

Tusi's formulation reflects the influence of a cultured, urban environment based on agriculture. Such a highly structured social order could hardly have characterized the early Ottomans. A mobile, frontier principality in Anatolia deriving its wealth from booty and flocks would not have a complex socioeconomic organization. Gregory Palamas, the archbishop of Salonika who was a prisoner of the Ottomans in 1355, described Orhon as a man not yet completely severed from his nomadic past.

---

*Nasir ad-Din Tusi, *The Nasirean Ethics*, G. M. Wickens (tr.) (London: George Allen and Unwin, 1964), p. 230.

Even at this early stage, however, dividing lines within the society did exist. One such major line of division separated nascent Ottoman society into two segments. In simplest terms we can call the two groups the rulers and the ruled. In Turkish they are called the *askeris* and *reaya*, which can be translated as "the military" and "the subjects." As the productive elements in society, the *reaya* produced the wealth that supported the military class. The *reaya* consisted of three categories: peasants, town and city dwellers, and nomads. The term encompassed both Muslims and non-Muslims. In post-Suleimanic times, however, the term came to designate mostly the non-Muslim subjects of the sultan. The *reaya* were further set apart from the *askeri* class by sumptuary laws that regulated their dress and prevented them from riding horses or carrying swords.

The rapid development of the *askeris* no doubt is connected with the Ottoman move into Europe in the first half of the fourteenth century and the resultant need for more cavalrymen and for administrators to organize the newly conquered territories. Sovereign power resided in the will of the sultan, but the practical necessities of governing an expanding state required the sultan to delegate some of his authority. Those who exercised that authority or served the sultan in other ways, and their families and their own retainers, all had *askeri* status. Their special position was surrounded with privileges, the most notable being important tax exemptions. The distinction between the *askeris* and the *reaya* was intended to be absolute, and the sultan could elevate a member of the *reaya* to *askeri* status only under extraordinary circumstances. The *askeris* zealously guarded their privileged position and looked to the sultan to maintain the dividing line between themselves and the rest of his subjects. Thus, the *askeri-reaya* division was a fundamental characteristic of Ottoman society.

The backbone of the *askeri* class was the vast group of men who constituted the Ottoman provincial cavalry. In return for their military service they were granted incomes derived from agricultural tax revenues collected from the provinces. Those incomes were called timars, and the men who held them were timariots, that is, timar-holders. Until the reign of Mohammed II most of the timar-holders were apparently men who had been born Muslims or who were the slaves of the sultans or the great military beys. An important number of Christians were also granted timars in that early period. These Christians were members of the Balkan military aristocracy who had thrown in their lot with the conquerors and thus managed to preserve their privileged status under the new Ottoman dispensation. Although they were under no compulsion to convert to Islam, they seem to have disappeared by the end of the fifteenth century. Perhaps the Christian timariots became aware that their future would be assured if they converted to Islam and thus became totally assimilated into the Ottoman *askeri* class; or perhaps the Ottoman willingness to accommodate the Christians within their own military establishment underwent a sharp turnabout. (A reversal in policy did occur after Christian revolts broke out in the Balkans in the first half of the fifteenth century.) It is most likely, however, that both of these factors were operative simultaneously.

Military and administrative organizations were both closely entwined with the timar system. By granting timars to their cavalrymen, the Ottoman sultans solved the problem of maintaining a large military force without huge outlays of cash. Since their economy suffered a chronic shortage of precious metals, paying their troops with timars rather than with cash relieved the central state treasury of an enormous burden. An added advantage of the timar system was that the timariots, in addition to carrying out their military duties on state campaigns, also performed important functions on the local level in the provincial administration.

PROVINCIAL STRUCTURE
The timariots usually resided in the villages that made up their holdings. Several of these villages comprised a sanjak, which was the basic administrative territorial unit. A sanjak was administered by the sanjakbeg, who was also its chief military officer. He was assisted by his lieutenants, who lived in the principal towns of the sanjak. For greater

administrative efficiency the work of all the sanjakbegs in a particular area was coordinated by an official called a beglerbeg, or "bey of the beys." The sanjaks under his control constituted a beglerbeglik. Murad I appointed the first beglerbeg in Rumeli in order to give greater cohesion to the expanding Ottoman drive in the Balkans. Thereafter Rumeli was the most prestigious beglerbeglik. For a while affairs in Anatolia continued to be directed personally by the sultan, but when Bajazet I began to devote more attention to expansion in Rumeli, he found that he needed someone to assume his authority in Anatolia. In 1393 the second beglerbeglik was formed in western Anatolia. Another was organized in central Anatolia early in the fifteenth century, as the Ottomans extended their control eastward. At the beginning of Suleiman's reign in 1520, the beglerbeglik of Rumeli had thirty sanjaks, and Anatolia had twenty. By 1609 there were thirty-two beglerbegliks. By that time the term "beglerbeglik" had been replaced by "eyalet," and beglerbegs were also known as "valis," or governors. (It is interesting to note that the Ottomans did not employ the term "empire" to denote their state. Instead, they used the expression *memalik-i mahrusa,* "the well-protected [by God] domains [of the sultan].")

The Cadastral Survey   Timar assignments were controlled by the central government and were dependent upon the provincial cadastral surveys. These surveys, known as *tahrirs,* were an essential instrument of Ottoman administration. They listed all sources of revenue, village by village, for each sanjak. Officials charged with the performance of the survey found out the names of all adult males who worked the land, the number of households in existence, types of crops and their yields over the past several years, and the amount of each crop collected as taxes, as well as the rate of all money levies made in the region. From this information a record was compiled of all the taxpayers and the sources of their income.

Tahrirs were initially carried out upon the conquest of a region and subsequently they could be undertaken for any of the following reasons: if a new sultan acceded to the throne; if a radical change, usually a diminution, occurred in the income derived from a sanjak; if the government desired to integrate into the tax structure any forms of wealth that had been overlooked in previous surveys; or if the government needed to take note of changes in personnel or property that may have occurred over time.

The register for the sanjak of Albania for the year 1431–1432 provides insight into the cadastral process. The region had been surveyed during the reigns of Bajazet I and Mohammed I. The survey of 1431–1432 was commanded by Sultan Murad II and carried out under the supervision of Umur Bey, the son of Saruca Pasha. When he arrived in Albania, Umur summoned before him all the timar-holders of the sanjak. They appeared with their documents, primarily letters of patent issued by the sultan, the beglerbeg, the sanjakbeg, or his lieutenant. The inspection was public, and the supervisor was assisted by the local kadis, or government officials trained in the religious law of Islam. The kadis' responsibilities included judicial matters and a wide variety of administrative functions on the local level. Two registers were produced from the information gathered by the commission. One was a detailed register that listed village by village the names of the heads of households, the amount of land they worked, and the total amount of revenue to be levied from each village through the tithe and other taxes. The first register also included the *kanun-name* for the sanjak. The *kanun-name* was a codification of the traditional taxes and the new Islamic taxes that applied to the sanjak and a list of regulations that not only spelled out the obligations of the *reaya*, but also set the limits on what the timar-holders could exact from them. Through the integration of local conditions into Ottoman legislation and the provision of legal protection for the *reaya*, the Ottomans facilitated the imposition of their rule. The second register was a summary register. In it were recorded all the timars in the sanjak with the names of their holders and often a statement on the past history of the timar: who had held it previously and how it had passed to the present holder. The timar-holder's military obligation, the villages constituting the timar, the number of households in each village, and the total revenue associated with the timar were also recorded. A copy of the summary register was usually kept by the beglerbeg, that is, by the military commander. In it he recorded changes in the status of the timars, such as the death of timar-holders and the reassignment of their timars. In that way the commander knew when his forces were up to full strength and when timars were vacant.

Timars were granted through the following procedure: a petitioner seeking a timar first secured a statement from the commander, the beglerbeg or the sanjakbeg, that he merited a timar. In response to such a petition an order was issued in the sultan's name to the effect that the petitioner was eligible for a timar, with an indication of the value of the timar to be granted. When the commander's records revealed that a timar in the stipulated amount was vacant, he issued an authorization for the timar to the petitioner. The sultan then granted the letter of patent for the timar. That was the general pattern, but there were many timar-holders in the pre-Suleimanic period who held their grants solely on the strength of certificates from their commanders. That practice had led to many abuses, including the admission of many of the *reaya* into the *askeri* class. Suleiman the Magnificent carried out a general review of timars, but despite his efforts at tightening the central government's control over the timar system, abuses still persisted.

Timars varied in value. Timar incomes of between 20,000 and 100,000 akchas were known as *zeamets*. (In the fifteenth and sixteenth centuries one gold ducat was worth between 50 and 60 akchas.) Holders of *zeamets* were called *zaims*, and they were high officers, usually lieutenants to the sanjakbegs. *Has* grants were worth more than 100,000 akchas, and the incomes were tied to the maintenance of specific offices, such as that of sanjakbeg, rather than to individuals. The holder of the office enjoyed the income from the *has* grant as long as he held that particular office. The Albanian sanjakbeg's *has* in the year 1431–1432 was worth the immense sum of over 250,000 akchas. *Has* grants were also set aside for the sultan to cover costs of the central government and to pay the salaries of high-ranking officials in the central administration. Eventually, *has* were also granted to palace favorites and even to women of the sultan's harem, but that development is characteristic of the timar system's corruption and ultimate demise.

Timars and Fighting Strength One of the major functions of the *tahrirs* and the timar system was to inform the sultan of the number of fighting men available to him. An analysis of the Argirikasri (modern Gjinokastër) subdivision of the sanjak of Albania provides an illustration of the way the system worked to supply the sultan with fighters and to keep him appraised of the strength of his forces. This example will also show what kinds of men made up a typical group of timariots. In 1432 Argirikasri was divided into one *has* and fifty-two timar grants, supporting sixty-nine timariots (several grants were held jointly by two or three men). The *has* grant was set aside for the maintenance of the sanjakbeg of Albania. His income was over 250,000 akchas a year, in return for which he had to provide thirty-two fully armed horsemen with cuirasses; in addition he also provided two suits of mail, three tents, and one field kitchen. Each cavalryman brought his own mounts and weapons, consisting of bow and arrows, sword, shield, and mace. Seventeen of the thirty-two timariots, whose grants averaged 1,200 akchas, contributed only their own service, mounted and fully armed; sixteen others, whose timars averaged 1,850 akchas, had accompanying them one slave each; and eight timariots, whose grants averaged 2,550 akchas, appeared with heavy armor, accompanied by another mounted warrior in light armor. Holders of timars with higher incomes were generally required to outfit one additional man for each 3,000 akchas of income, as can be seen in the following excerpt from the register:

The timar of Sunkur, a slave of the bey. In the time of the late sultan it supported the steward Murad. In our [the present] sultan's reign they gave it to the aforementioned [Sunkur]. He possesses the sultan's patent.

Himself in heavy armor, 4 horsemen with cuirasses, 1 tent

[Then follows village by village the number of households and income from each village]

Total: 8 villages, 2 cultivated sites, 171 households, 8 widows, 6 bachelors

Revenue . . . 12,671 akchas

Argirikasri's total contribution to the sanjak's cavalry force was 134 men, 7 tents, 2 coats of mail, and 1 field kitchen. The heaviest military burden fell on those with the highest incomes. This equitable system provided the sultan with a fighting force that was the scourge of Europe and the Near East into the seventeenth century. The timar system enabled Mohammed the Conqueror to put into the field some 34,000 timariots from all of his domains, and Suleiman the Magnificent, even with the newly conquered Arab provinces exempt from the timar system, close to 40,000.

The group of timar-holders of Argirikasri reveals many characteristics of the *askeri* class under the early sultans. Three timariots were Christians. Other Christian timarholders had converted to Islam or had slipped down into the *reaya* class. Twelve timariots were former slaves. This pattern of mobility was typical for men who had been enslaved captives or prisoners of war and who later were rewarded for their service by the grant of timars. Eighteen men possessed timars previously held by their fathers. Those timars were not willed to them by their fathers, for timars were revocable grants given by the sultan through the central government and were not the personal property of the timariots. In theory all land, except religious endowments and the small amount that had been allowed to become private holdings, belonged to the sultan. He allowed others certain rights on the land; for example, the timar-holder enjoyed a share in the revenue from the land in return for his service. As members of the *askeri* class, however, sons of timar-holders were eligible for and were often granted their fathers' timars. The value of such a timar would vary according to the value of the parent's timar and whether or not the parent had died in combat. Sons of timariots tended to follow their fathers into the timariot category and to stay there. Rarely did an ordinary timar-holder rise to prominence in any other field of service within the *askeri* class. In the sixteenth century this procedure had a salutary effect: the number of sons succeeding to grants held by their fathers or receiving grants in their own right ensured the necessary element of stability to the timar system.

PROVINCIAL ADMINISTRATION
Stability was crucial since the timariots were part of the Ottoman administrative apparatus as well as the military. The administrative hierarchy copied the military one: the sultan's authority was passed down from the beglerbeg through the sanjakbeg and his lieutenant to the ordinary timariot. The beglerbeg, with the rank of vizier and the title of pasha, exercised his control over the sanjaks in his province through a council (divan) that was a microcosm of the sultan's governmental machinery in the capital. He was assisted by financial officers, secretaries, and personal aides in dealing with assignment and promotion of timar-holders, legal suits involving members of the *askeri* class, remittance to the capital of revenues collected on behalf of the central treasury, and execution of all commands issued by the sultan. Only about one-third of the revenues collected in a province were assigned as timars. Much of the remainder was set aside for the sultan, who used it to meet the expenses of the central government. Furthermore, the capitation tax, or head tax, levied on non-Muslims was collected for the central treasury. The beglerbeg was expected to administer his province, meet all expenses out of incoming revenues, and remit the surplus to the capital for use in defraying the costs of the central government. It was assumed that there would be a surplus, and for a remarkably long time such was the case. Not until the seventeenth century did the central government regularly find expenditures outstripping receipts. That state of affairs, of course, is intimately bound up with the empire's decline.

On the village level the timariots assisted in the collection of taxes and in the maintenance of public security, which involved ridding the area of brigands. Peaceful and continual cultivation of the land and payment of taxes

47

were fundamental objectives of the central government. To achieve these objectives the timariot was delegated authority to see that the peasants remained on the land and worked it as stipulated. He could pursue those who left and compel them to return, and he was encouraged to settle more peasants and bring more land under cultivation. The peasants had hereditary usufructuary rights on the land, in return for which they paid the tithe and an annual tax of 22 akchas per unit of land. The basic land unit was defined as the amount of land that could be ploughed in one day by a pair of oxen. That unit eventually was fixed at approximately one-quarter of an acre. This hearth tax represented the conversion into a cash payment of the seven goods and services (such as transportation of hay and firewood and corvée on the lord's estates), which the peasants formerly owed the lord under Byzantine rule. This tax was one way in which the Ottomans made their regime less oppressive for the peasants than that of their predecessors. Another way was to detail in the provincial administrative regulations the responsibilities of the peasants toward the timariot and to spell out their symbiotic relationship. When abuses materialized the peasants had recourse to the kadi's court for redress. In extremities they could even petition the sultan directly.

Two observations are in order at this point with respect to the Ottoman system of *tahrirs* and timars. The first is that the system gave the empire an important element of continuity. It had been the basic administrative technique of Persian statecraft and had been given its Islamic character under the Great Seljuks in Persia in the mid-eleventh century. The system was passed on to the Ottomans through the Seljuks of Rum, and the Ottomans did not abandon it until the nineteenth century. Continuity in this and other basic institutions reveals and underscores the essentially conservative character of Islamic society. It was this conservatism that devitalized the society, rather than the acceptance of the role of fate (kismet) in the affairs of men (a familiar but misleading generalization). Second, it would be a mistake to equate the timar system with western European feudalism, similar as they may appear. In the absence of strong central authority European feudalism provided for government at the local level with justice dispensed by local lords and ties of vassalage descending through several levels of subinfeudation. The Ottoman system, on the other hand, had a strong central government at its heart. One of the sultan's principal functions was the dispensation of justice, and the timariots had no authority to decide legal matters in private courts. Also, the timariots were not bound by any ties of vassalage, and subinfeudation had no place in the Ottoman system.

THE GHULAM
SYSTEM

Another institution characteristic of the Ottomans and one that further sets them off from any Western European feudal model is the *ghulam* system. A *ghulam* was a slave highly trained for service in the ruler's palace and state structure. *Ghulams* in the service of Muslim rulers came into importance in Islamic history as early as the reign of Caliph al-Mutasim (833–842). As with many of their institutions, the Ottomans had as their model the *ghulam* practice of the Seljuks of Rum. Although even the earliest Ottoman rulers had their slaves, the systematic training and employment of *ghulams* is associated with the development of the janissary corps and the introduction of the *devshirme*, the well-known levy of Christian youths. The janissaries were the elite, well-trained, Ottoman standing infantry corps. They are said to have been first organized in the reign of Murad I from the one-fifth share of the booty, including prisoners, allotted to the sultan by the religious law of Islam. Prisoners of war, however, provided neither a steady nor a properly trainable supply of slaves. To solve this problem the Ottomans hit upon the idea of taking into their service and converting to Islam the young male children of their Christian subjects. This periodic levy, known as the *devshirme* (from the Turkish verb meaning "to collect"), was an Ottoman innovation in the *ghulam* system, but the precise date of its inception is still unknown. It would appear, however, that the Ottomans were already training *devshirme* boys as early at 1395.

Devshirme   The youths were collected as an extraordinary tax levied on the sultan's authority alone, without any reference to the religious law. Size and frequency of the levies varied according to the needs of the government. Heavy losses in personnel, sustained over several campaigning seasons, would necessitate larger or more frequent levies. An extraordinary tax, the levy was assessed against an entire village or number of villages constituting the special "tax-units" organized for such taxes, rather than on individual households. That practice tended to make the burden more equitable. The number of youths taken generally averaged one for every forty households. Seeking hardy, trainable subjects, the Ottomans took only unmarried village youths between the ages of about eight and eighteen years (in the seventeenth century the limits appear to have been fifteen to twenty years). At first boys were taken only from the Balkans, but later, in the sixteenth century, they were levied from Anatolia as well. Certain categories of boys were exempt, however, including only sons, boys with trades vital to the local economy, orphans, and known behavior problems.

In the sixteenth century, when a *devshirme* had been decided upon, janissary officers armed with an authorization from the sultan proceeded to the sanjaks being subjected to the levy. They set up in the large towns and sent criers to the villages to notify local officials, including the kadis and the timar-holders. Fathers were told to bring their sons in for inspection, and they were accompanied by the priests, who brought along the baptismal records. The janissary officers then examined the youths. The name, age, parentage, residence, and description of each boy selected was recorded in a register, of which a duplicate copy was made. The chosen boys were then collected in groups of 100 to 150, dressed in special garments, and dispatched to Istanbul in the care of a janissary escort, who was entrusted with one copy of the register, the other copy remaining with the collecting officer. At headquarters in Istanbul, after all the youths were collected, the two registers were compared to ensure that no substitutions had been made en route, because it was common knowledge that some parents sought to buy their children out of the levy. Later, when the personal advantages offered by the *devshirme* had become evident, others would try to buy their sons in.

In the capital the boys, who would soon be converted to Islam and circumcised, were put through a series of examinations to determine their capabilities. Physiognomy played an important role in the screening process, as did phrenology. The best physical specimens, perhaps one in ten, were siphoned off immediately for training in the palaces of Istanbul and Edirne. These boys were destined for the finest education available in the Islamic world and were prepared for the highest positions in the empire. The vast majority of those collected, however, were hired out to Turkish farmers in Anatolia and Rumeli, where they would learn Turkish and become familiar with the Islamic faith. Regular checks were kept on their progress, and when they were ready or needed they were brought back to Istanbul and enrolled in the ranks of the janissaries. The janissaries numbered 6,000 toward the end of Mohammed the Conqueror's reign, close to 8,000 at the beginning of Suleiman's reign, and 12,000 when he died in 1566. By 1609 the corps had burgeoned to 37,000.

Chikma   The chosen few selected for the palace were subjected to a rigorous and regimented educational program under the supervision of palace eunuchs. At the beginning of the sixteenth century there were some three hundred boys in the palace at Edirne. This first step in their training lasted from two to eight years, and at the end of that initial period they were again reviewed. The most outstanding were destined for further training at Topkapi Sarayi, the sultan's residence in Istanbul. Those who failed to qualify for promotion were usually assigned high-ranking positions in units of the sultan's salaried household cavalry, the *Sipahis* of the Porte. This process of selection and advancement, which was an integral part of the Ottoman *ghulam* system, was termed the *chikma*, or "graduation." In the sixteenth century a *chikma* occurred about once every two to five years, and in the seventeenth century every seven or eight years. Usually a *chikma* also took place upon the accession of a new sultan.

The Inner Service   Within the departments of the Inner Service at Topkapi palace, the newly promoted pages were prepared for their future positions. The Inner Service was a series of chambers and departments devoted to the personal service of the sultan, and it was the environment in which he passed much of his private life. The first two chambers—perhaps "college" would be a better term—were the small chamber and the great chamber, where the pages of the Inner Service devoted themselves to studies and physical training. Estimates of the number of pages in training in the first half of the sixteenth century vary from 600 to 700. When compared with the total number of janissaries and household cavalry—12,000 in 1527 and 58,000 in 1609—the elitist character of the Inner Service is evident. Education in the Inner Service transmitted the High Islamic tradition to these new converts to Islam. They were trained in the Koran and associated religious sciences. They learned Arabic, Persian, Turkish, music, calligraphy, and mathematics. So that physical qualities would not be neglected, they were also schooled in the warrior skills of horsemanship, archery, wrestling, and the handling of personal weapons. In addition, each page acquired a professional artistic skill such as miniature painting or bookbinding.

The Outer Service   After some four years in the first two chambers the pages were again put through a weeding-out process. The most deserving were admitted to the senior chambers, where they were trained for personal attendance upon the sultan. Places were found in the household cavalry for those who had to leave the palace. They left the palace with handsome salaries, for in the course of their training the pages had received stipends that increased with their progress. Those who continued in the palace were eventually promoted to agaships on the basis of seniority and efficiency, the twin principles that governed the *ghulam* system. The agas managed and directed palace affairs, and the highest-ranking agas had access to the sultan, thus enabling them to influence matters of state. Senior pages who were not promoted to agaships left the Inner Service for the Outer Service. As the name implies, the Outer Service involved the affairs of the empire outside the sultan's palace. Since the Ottoman state was committed to conquest, it is not surprising to find that the departments composing the Outer Service were intimately concerned with military matters. Those departments included janissaries, household cavalry, artillery, palace guards, quartermasters, armorers, falconers, stable personnel, and craftsmen such as swordmakers. Mohammed the Conqueror's power rested on his slave organization, the slaves of the Porte, which he built up through the *ghulam* system to counterbalance the power of the frontier lords. Mohammed structured the organization and in his law code, the *kanun-name* of Mohammed II, defined the order of precedence for each position. The agas who headed those departments were called the agas of the stirrup and rode to campaign beside the sultan. When the agas of the stirrup left the Outer Service they assumed posts as governors of provinces or at the least as sanjakbegs. Lesser agas became lieutenants to sanjakbegs and received large incomes. In this manner the *chikma* served to weld the principal institutions of the state, the timar and *ghulam* systems, into an integrated whole. The timars provided the basic manpower for the cavalry and the local personnel for the administrative apparatus. The *devshirme* also provided a good portion of the fighting forces, as well as *ghulams*. *Ghulams* who graduated from the palace provided the leadership as governors, sanjakbegs, and their subalterns; and others in the Inner and Outer services led the military and palace establishments. In 1453 Mahmud Pasha, who was a product of the *ghulam* system, was appointed Mohammed II's grand vizier to succeed Chandarli Halil, who represented the religious establishment and the previously entrenched aristocratic Muslim families. From that time until the eighteenth century, and with very few exceptions, *ghulams* controlled that supreme administrative office in the empire.

The career of Lufti Pasha, who served as one of Suleiman the Magnificent's grand viziers, is illustrative of the manner in which the *ghulam* system functioned. He had entered the palace during the reign of Bajazet II. After his instructional period he rose through the chambers to be a royal footman. At the accession of Selim I in 1512, he left the Inner Service for a position in the Outer Service with one of the elite guards units, receiving a daily salary of 50 akchas, the equivalent of a *zeamet* grant. After serving in several agaships of the Outer Service, including duty as a chief gatekeeper of the palace, he became sanjakbeg of Kastamonu in Anatolia. Eventually he became beglerbeg of Anatolia and attained the rank of vizier. In 1539 he achieved the pinnacle of power as grand vizier to Suleiman.

THE GRAND VIZIER AND THE DIVAN

The grand vizier was the sultan's deputy in all matters of state. Early sultans had personally conducted meetings of their divan, or council, but Mohammed II late in his reign withdrew from that arduous task and left the day-to-day conduct of state business to his grand vizier. He did, however, have a small grille cut into the wall of the council chamber, which stood in the second courtyard of the Topkapi palace in Istanbul. Behind the grille he could listen to discussions and intervene when matters required it. Succeeding sultans tended to follow his lead, although at times some preferred to preside over the council meetings and thus again concentrate control of state affairs in their own hands. Meetings of the imperial divan during the sixteenth century were held on Saturday, Sunday, Monday, and Tuesday. On Sundays and Tuesdays decisions were presented to the sultan for his approval. In the second half of the seventeenth century much of the grand vizier's work was done in special council meetings held at his official residence.

Under the direction of the grand vizier the imperial divan dealt with all governmental matters. The imperial divan was made up of the highest executive and military officers and several administrative and procedural officials, including the chief financial officer and his two assistants, the chief judicial officers for Rumeli and Anatolia, and a group of viziers who were known as the viziers of the dome (because their place at the meeting was under a dome). That composition reflected the Ottoman division of state affairs into military (which included governmental administration), judicial, and financial. Others who attended the imperial divan included the official who checked government documents and affixed the sultan's royal signet to them, indicating that the document conformed to state regulations and to the religious law; the janissary commander; the chief admiral; and the chief of state bureaucracy (*reisülküttab*). Final decision in all matters discussed in the divan rested with the grand vizier, who would then give an account of his stewardship to the sultan and secure his consent to all decisions. Symbol of the grand vizier's authority was the seal of office entrusted to him by the sultan. A sign of his removal from office was repossession of the seal, which was then broken.

THE
BUREAUCRACY

Supporting the divan was a bureaucratic structure that helped in implementing decisions and keeping the state records. The paperwork generated in this highly centralized, bureaucratic empire was immense. In the sixteenth century the central bureaucracy was composed of two principal sections, the bureaus of the imperial divan and the bureaus of the financial administration. Three bureaus comprised central administration under the divan. The first bureau, known as the Bureau of the Divan, was concerned with the drafting, issuance, and filing of all decrees, edicts, and regulations other than those dealing with finances, including documents relating to foreign affairs, such as treaties and capitulations. (In European governments this bureau would be the equivalent of the chancery office.) The other two bureaus of the divan were concerned with personnel. They kept the records of appointments of viziers, kadis, and provincial officers, such as governors and sanjakbegs. They also recorded all matters relating to the assignment of timars. In effect, all appointments to positions in the three divisions of the government, military, bureaucratic, and religious affairs, were handled in these two bureaus. The chief officer of the central administration was the *reisülküttab*, or "chief of the scribes," who was to emerge in the late seventeenth and eighteenth centuries as the official most concerned with foreign relations. In the nineteenth century his office would be called the Ministry for Foreign Affairs.

The bureaus of the financial administration were many more in number, totaling some twenty-five in the late eighteenth century. They were concerned with all matters related to income and expenditures. Income was derived primarily from taxes levied on religious authority and from taxes, duties, and tolls levied by the authority of the state. Expenditures were concerned mainly with salaries and with what today would be considered national defense. The financial administration was presided over by the chief financial officer and his two principal assistants, with the *reisülküttab* in charge of the bureau secretaries.

In time of campaign many of the bureaucratic personnel, from both central and financial divisions, accompanied the army into the field to accomplish the paperwork necessitated by warfare. At those times deputies for the principal officers were appointed who superintended the work of the bureaus in the capital. This practice was especially important in the case of the grand vizier, who often assumed the role of commander-in-chief after the middle of the sixteenth century, when the sultans generally refrained from campaigning personally.

Unlike the *ghulam* system, the bureaucracy during the reign of Suleiman was staffed almost completely by men who were born Muslims. More and more the bureaucrats tended to be sons or other relatives of secretaries themselves. They were trained in the bureaus by the chief permanent secretaries, within a system that resembled the European guild organization with its master-apprentice relationships. Upon entering the bureaus in their early teens, the apprentices were taught their trade, which included the various scripts used in official correspondence, the format of various state documents, and the other elements of expertise necessary for success in the scribal profession. Following mornings of professional instruction, the apprentices and the secretaries would attend afternoon courses in the leading mosques of Istanbul in order to complete their more traditional Muslim education, with the aim of becoming well-rounded Muslim gentlemen. Bureaus were staffed by apprentices in various stages of training, by secretaries, and by permanent, or senior, secretaries, all under the bureau chief. The bureau chiefs, known as the *hacegân,* constituted the broad upper bracket of the Ottoman bureaucracy. Below the *hacegân* level, bureaucrats tended to spend their entire careers within a single bureau unless they managed to exhibit special talent or found a patron to further their careers. A bureau chief, on the other hand, usually served as the head of a bureau for a year or two and then moved on to direct another bureau. This system for the training of a professional bureaucratic class had its roots in the Persian traditions of statecraft. As in the case of other institutions which were derived from earlier Islamic practices, the Ottomans refined the bureaucracy and developed it to new heights.

JUSTICE   Another fundamental feature of the imperial divan was its role in the dispensation of justice. One of the traditional main functions of the sovereign in Near Eastern states, both pre-Islamic and Islamic, was to ensure that justice reigned throughout the land. Symbolic of this was the "tower of justice," a high structure from which the ruler could theoretically observe any act of tyranny being committed by any of his officials. The sultan would have the official apprehended and punished and the wrong righted. Ottoman practices demonstrated the sultans' attachment to this ancient view of sovereignty. These practices included the construction of a "tower of justice" in the Topkapi palace, the granting of wishes to petitioners who managed to touch the hem of the sultan's robe, the holding of extraordinary audiences to hear complaints, and, of course, the dedication of the divan itself to the rectification of grievances caused by officials who misused the authority delegated to them. Justice was dispensed in the sultan's name by the grand vizier in the divan, with the chief judges of Rumeli and Anatolia rendering decisions on matters pertaining to the religious law. The chief judges headed the ulema, as the religious establishment was known. In the sixteenth century, however, the chief judges were overshadowed by the sheikh ul-Islam, a dignitary who originally was outside the official ulema hierarchy. His position as an "outsider" was intended to enhance the objectivity of his decisions on questions of religious law. He was, in effect, supposed to function as an independent judicial authority, a sort of supreme court, above the pressures of everyday official life. Gradually, the sheikh ul-Islam came to control the ulema organization, with authority to appoint kadis and staff members in the empire-wide religious educational institutions. Despite the increase in his real power, the sheikh ul-Islam did not attain a seat in the imperial divan, whose meetings he attended only by invitation under extraordinary circumstances. The career of Ebüssund, powerful sheikh ul-Islam under Suleiman the Magnificent, illustrates the career pattern of a sheikh ul-Islam: He was born in 1490 and educated in the mosque schools. Upon the completion of his education he became a teacher and eventually taught in the Ottoman version of an Ivy League school, the mosque school of Mohammed the Conqueror in Istanbul. In 1533 he became a kadi, serving in Bursa and Istanbul. By 1537 he was chief judge of Rumeli, and in 1545 he was appointed sheikh ul-Islam. He held that position until his death in 1574.

The Ottoman Empire's basic institutions and organizations described so far approximated the model of the ideal Islamic society set forth by Nasireddin Tusi. The *askeri* class, consisting of the privileged members of society who performed the military, administrative, and religious function within the Ottoman state, would correspond to Tusi's first two classes, the Men of the Sword and the Men of the Pen. The *reaya* would encompass his last two classes, the Men of Negotiation and the Men of Husbandry—that is, the tradespeople and the peasants. In the nearly two hundred years that passed between the rise of the Ottomans and the reign of Suleiman the Magnificent two crucial changes took place as Ottoman society became more sophisticated and complex.

Thorough Islamization of the *askeri* class was the first of those changes. With the disappearance of the Christian timar-holders, the indispensable condition for membership in the *askeri* class was to profess the faith of Islam. Timar-holders, bureaucrats, ulema, and slaves of the Porte were Muslims, either by birth or by conversion. Neither path to the true faith was preferred over the other.

The *reaya*, on the other hand, consisted of both Muslims and non-Muslims. A major distinction between the two was the fact that the Muslim *reaya* did not have to pay the capitation tax. Another distinction was that the *reaya* were organized into legally recognized religious communities known as millets. Personal identity in the premodern, pre-nation-state Near East was by religion, and even by sect. The main millets were the Greek Christians, the Armenian Christians, and the Jews. Each millet had its own organization under its religious leaders. Individual millet members related to the central government through their millet, which was responsible for, among other things, tax allocations and collection, community education, and intracommunal legal matters, especially those dealing with personal status, such as marriage, divorce, and inheritance. The Muslims were not a millet, but rather considered themselves as the community of Muhammad. In the societal pecking order the Muslim *reaya*, although clearly not as well off politically, socially, or financially as the Muslims in the *askeri* class, still felt themselves superior to their non-Muslim fellow *reaya*, identifying with the sultan and the success of the Ottoman cause in its struggles with the infidels.

THE TRUE
OTTOMANS

The second change was the dual process of diversification and stratification that took place within the *askeri* class. By the reign of Suleiman the *askeri* class was composed of men who served the sultan within clearly defined careers—military, bureaucracy, and religion. The bureaucratic and the religious careers correspond to Tusi's first social class, the Men of the Pen. He grouped together scribes, kadis, and teachers in a single class. In pre-Ottoman Islamic societies, however, and even in early Ottoman times, the distinction between scribes and ulema was not so sharply drawn. In that early period it makes sense to consider the ulema an undifferentiated group that supplied the state with both its scribes and its religious functionaries. Only as the nature of those official positions became more specialized and complex did separate careers develop, with their own systems of education and sources of manpower. More and more those sources tended to be the families of men already in those careers. Sons quickly followed in the footsteps of their fathers, to the applause of a society that believed in the value expressed in the proverb: "A son who resembles his father does no injustice." This tendency was true in each of the three careers. It was most noticeable in the religious career, only slightly less so in the bureaucracy, and toward the end of Suleiman's era it also was becoming apparent in the military. For the military, that tendency constituted a serious blow to the very nature of the *ghulam* system. The *devshirme* and the palace educational enterprise were designed to prepare people for the sultan's service who placed nothing else above his cause. For highly placed officials in the military to preempt positions for their own sons was to undermine seriously one of the state's fundamental pillars by making the family more important than the sultan.

These processes taking place within the *askeri* class ultimately divided that ruling class into two segments. The line along which the cleavage took place was education. Career specializations and the education necessary for success in a chosen career combined to produce within the broader *askeri* class an elite whose members deserve to be called the true Ottomans. The term "Ottoman" here has a meaning not merely dynastic, but also cultural. The Ottomans were a small minority in the *askeri* class, for, to be an Ottoman, one had to satisfy three conditions: serve the state; serve the religion; and "know the Ottoman Way." Serving the state meant working for the government in a position that gave the privileged status associated with the *askeri* class. Serving the religion simply meant being a Muslim. "Knowing the Ottoman Way" involved being completely conversant with the High Islamic cultural tradition, including being at home in the Turkish language (for which a knowledge of Arabic and Persian was also necessary) and conforming in public to the conventional manners and customs for which that speech was the vehicle.

SOCIAL
MOBILITY

Class barriers in the Ottoman society were not insurmountable, and there were many avenues open for those bent on becoming true Ottomans. For someone born a non-Muslim below the status of *askeri*, the path to Ottoman status would involve first becoming a Muslim and then moving upward from *reaya* to *askeri* through education and one of the three careers. This objective was most simply accomplished through the *devshirme*. A boy levied in the *devshirme* would become a Muslim, and, if fortunate enough to be chosen for service in the palace, he would ultimately find a place in the military hierarchy well within the Ottoman elite. At the very least, such a boy would become a janissary and thus be one of the *askeri* class. For a Muslim boy born in the *reaya*, the problem was both simpler and more difficult. He was already on the right side of the religious divide, and all he had to do was rise. Rising, however, was not as easy for the Muslim as it was for the prospective *devshirme* candidate. The upward climb for the Muslim youth usually involved finding an Ottoman sponsor early enough to make the proper education feasible. Entrance into the *askeri* class might be accomplished simply by volunteering for campaign in the hope of displaying courage and being rewarded with the grant of a timar. Sons born to men already in the Ottoman elite were clearly well ahead of the field. Their fathers would see to their education and had the necessary connections to launch their offspring on Ottoman careers. In general, sons of men of the *askeri* class already had *askeri* status. To attain Ottoman status they would merely have to cross the educational barrier. Evidence indicates that, in the main, the Ottoman elite replenished itself from within its own ranks. This custom was not without significant implications for the unfolding of Ottoman history in the post-Suleimanic age.

Chapter 3

The
Post-Suleimanic Age

Heavy responsibilities as the world's leading Islamic power coupled with their tradition of ghazi idealism continued to motivate Ottoman actions in the post-Suleimanic age. Several significant differences are discernible, however, with respect to some of the regions in which the empire became heavily involved and the degree of success that crowned Ottoman efforts. Russia, North Africa, and the Mediterranean more and more became the focal points of Ottoman concern, and increasingly success was purchased at higher costs, and then ultimately not at all. Failure, for a polity and society predicated upon, committed to, and organized for conquest, was to have far-reaching and eventually devastating consequences. In 1603 the Ottoman Empire was characterized by the English historian Richard Knolles as "the present terror of the world"; by the second half of the nineteenth century the empire would become, in the words of Tsar Nicholas II of Russia, "the sick man of Europe."

THE MUSCOVY MENACE

In the 1530s, when the Ottomans first awoke to the threat posed by Muscovy, none of those symptoms that would lead the Tsar to make his diagnosis of the empire's state of health were yet evident. Relations between the Ottoman state and the Grand Duchy of Muscovy had been cordial up to that period. Imposition of Ottoman suzerainty over the Crimea in 1475 did not adversely affect the Ottoman-Muscovy relationship, and in 1492 the Russians were granted the privilege to trade freely in Ottoman domains. Ottoman suspicions were aroused in the 1530s, however, when the Russians sought to expand their influence over the entire Volga River basin. Those suspicions were soon confirmed. While Suleiman was preoccupied with extending Ottoman control over Moldavia in the eastern Black Sea area, Ivan IV (1533–1584) of Moscow moved against the remaining, enfeebled Tartar khanates in the Volga region. He took control of Kazan in 1552, and Astrakhan in 1556. The Russian aggression disrupted the pilgrimage traffic through Astrakhan and the lucrative northern trade routes, and the local Muslim population, as well as the Muslim rulers in Bukhara and Samarkand in Turkestan, sent pleas to the Ottoman sultan, the champion of Islam, to assist them in opposing the aggressor.

In Istanbul the imperial divan considered how the empire should respond to the pleas. Devlet Giray, the khan of the Crimea, counseled an immediate attack upon Moscow itself. His suggestion was audacious but not impossible, for the Crimean Tartars had sacked Moscow in the past. The Tartars' views were considered in the divan, since they constituted a major element among the Ottoman fighting forces. In this instance, however, a counterproposal that was supported by Grand Vizier Sokollu carried the day. The plan that was adopted called for a strike against Astrakhan, together with a project to construct a canal linking the Don and Volga rivers, thus creating an all-water route from the Black Sea to the Caspian. If successful, this ambitious project would not only shut the Russians out of the Volga basin, but would also enable the Ottomans to dominate Georgia and the Caucasus and threaten Persia as well.

The canal project, though strategically sound, soon proved to be a logistical and tactical nightmare. An expeditionary force of ten thousand fighting men, three thousand Tartars, and six thousand laborers set out from the

Crimea in June 1569. Digging on the canal began late in August at Perevolok, the point on the Don closest to the Volga, but had to be abandoned. The Ottoman commander then decided to attack Astrakhan before winter set in. That project also failed, and the demoralized Ottomans withdrew to Azov. Winter exacted a heavy toll on the troops and much materiel, including artillery, had to be left behind. It became obvious that the Ottomans could not wage war successfully against the Russians in the inhospitable north, so far from their main bases of operation. The Ottoman sultans turned from the north and concentrated on the Mediterranean Sea and North Africa, leaving the burden of resistance to the Russians on the khan of the Crimea.

CONFLICT IN NORTH AFRICA

In the 1530s, at the same time the Muscovite threat first appeared, Ottoman penetration into North Africa began in earnest. After their conquest of Egypt in 1517, the Ottomans started to look westward. They gave logistical support to the independent Muslim corsairs operating against the Christians out of North African ports. Principal among these sea ghazis was Khair ed-Din Barbarossa. When the Hapsburgs under Charles V shifted their attention from Central Europe to the Mediterranean, Sultan Suleiman responded by setting his own naval establishment in order. He appointed Barbarossa grand admiral of the Ottoman fleet in 1534. Barbarossa in turn brought the previously independent Muslim corsairs under Ottoman suzerainty. North Africa and the western Mediterranean became a frontier zone in which Christians and Muslims contested for dominance, just as the Ottoman and Hapsburg empire boundary was contested on land.

The Hapsburgs, locked in an obdurate maritime struggle with their Muslim foes, established a defensive line from Sicily to Tunisia that included the fortresses of Tunis and Tripoli. The Ottomans pecked away at that line, taking Tripoli in 1551 and defeating a large Hapsburg fleet in 1560. Suleiman's last effort in the Mediterranean was the unsuccessful siege of Malta in 1565, a year before his death. The war party that gained ascendancy in Istanbul under his successor, Selim II, supported a forward policy in the western Mediterranean. A protégé of Grand Vizier Mohammed Sokollu Pasha was appointed governor of Algeria. That governor and the central government were keenly interested in the Morisco rebellion that broke out in Granada and the Protestant rebellion in the Netherlands.

That the Ottomans were aware of the difficulties the Hapsburgs were having with the Moriscos in Spain and with the Protestants in the Netherlands illustrates how well informed they were about the political affairs of Europe. Such information was gleaned from a variety of sources, including foreign ambassadors resident in Istanbul, renegades who had taken refuge in the empire, foreign merchants and travelers, and, in the instance of Spain, directly from the Moriscos themselves. That the Ottomans were concerned with these religious matters highlights the continuity in their policy. Earlier they had encouraged the Lutherans and the Calvinists in Central Europe; now it was the Moriscos and the Dutch Protestants. Behind this support was the hope that they would find political allies among the Christian religious dissenters.

Selim II sent his coreligionists in Granada fine words, but he was not able to supply any meaningful military assistance, because his attention was riveted on two objectives closer at hand and more immediately realizable than any chimerical Muslim reconquest of Spain. Those objectives were the island of Cyprus and the city of Tunis. In January 1570 Tunis fell to the Ottoman forces, and attention then focused on Cyprus. In Venetian hands since 1489, Cyprus had become a base for Christian corsairs operating against Ottoman communication lines with Egypt. The pirates also jeopardized the safety of pilgrims traveling in the eastern Mediterranean. Selim launched the attack on Cyprus in July 1570; Nicosia fell in September and Famagusta in August of the following year. The Hapsburgs, concerned with internal revolt in Granada and harassed by the Protestant uprising in the Netherlands, could not contribute to the allied Christian fleet that had sought to relieve the island.

Don Juan of Austria defeated the Moriscos in the autumn

of 1570, and the Hapsburgs were free once again to respond to the growing Ottoman menace in the Mediterranean. The Pope chose Don Juan to head the combined Christian fleet (mainly Spanish, Venetian, and Genoese) to resist the Ottoman advance. On October 7, 1571, a great naval battle, the last great clash of galley fleets in European history, was fought off the Greek town of Lepanto. The result was a splendid victory for the Christians. All Christendom rejoiced. Western historians have since considered the battle of Lepanto a crucial turning point in Mediterranean history, because the Christians now felt they had lifted the Ottoman cloak of invincibility. The Ottomans, however, were far from destroyed as a sea power. Selim II had the fleet rebuilt, drawing upon all available imperial resources, especially the skilled Algerian craftsmen and seamen. In 1573 the Venetians, sailing out to retake Cyprus, were surprised by a powerful new Ottoman fleet and withdrew. Venice, impoverished by the war, sought peace, and a treaty was signed that same year between the two powers that recognized the Ottoman conquest of Cyprus.

Spain, less concerned than Venice with commercial matters and more imbued with crusading zeal, challenged the Ottomans anew in North Africa. Don Juan retook Tunis in 1573, but in the following year the Ottomans again invested the city. The victory was announced around the Muslim world in an effort to refurbish the Ottoman ghazi image, which had been tarnished by the defeat at Lepanto. The Ottomans extended the sanjak structure and timar system to much of North Africa and continued their expansion westward. That expansionist policy was pressed on by Murad III (1574–1595), who succeeded Selim II. Working with indigenous Muslim dynasts, the Ottomans quickly sought to bring Morocco under their sway. In 1576 their client unseated the reigning sultan in Fez. With this victory Murad's name was recited in the Friday prayers and stamped on coinage, two traditional signs of sovereignty in the Islamic world.

The Ottoman success in Morocco awakened fears in Portugal. Now only the Straits of Gibraltar separated the Ottomans from the Iberian Peninsula. Philip II of Spain, in financial trouble, sought to come to terms with them so that he could be free to pursue his designs against England. Murad III postponed the final agreement, hoping to gain a position of greater strength in the negotiations by establishing a foothold in Iberia itself. Don Sebastian of Portugal therefore assumed the brunt of the Christian anti-Ottoman burden. The question was resolved on the battlefield of Alcazar on August 4, 1578. It was a costly encounter in which the three main contenders in Morocco, the Ottoman-supported sultan, the deposed sultan, and Don Sebastian, all met their death. Following that debacle, Philip II refused to become embroiled in Moroccan affairs, leaving the field open to the Ottomans. A formal peace between Philip and the Ottomans in August 1580 signaled recognition of that fact.

In retrospect, the battle of Alcazar and the peace of 1580 form a significant milestone in the relations between the Ottomans and the Hapsburgs and, by extension, in the history of Muslim and Christian relations in the western Mediterranean. After 1580 Morocco became the buffer zone between the two competing civilizations. North Africa remained Muslim, and the Iberian peninsula, protected by the Straits of Gibraltar, remained Christian, free from internal revolt after the final expulsion of the Moriscos in 1607, and secure from the threat of Ottoman invasion. Philip II was now at liberty to embark upon his English and Portuguese ventures, and the Ottomans themselves had more pressing business in the East.

CONFLICT IN THE EAST
The Ottomans had long opposed the development of any powerful state on their eastern flank. In defense of this flank, Bajazet I had clashed with Timur, Mohammed the Conqueror had destroyed Uzun Hasan, and Selim I and Suleiman had campaigned long and hard against the Safavids. In the case of the Safavids the danger was twofold, political and religious. The Safavids were both a militant state and an heretical Shi'ite sect. Religious propaganda, emanating from Persia and directed toward the nomads and peasants in eastern Anatolia, undermined Ottoman authority among disaffected elements. That propaganda

was spread by the shah's missionary agents, who also took up financial contributions to support the Shi'ite cause. It is characteristic of Islamic society that social, economic, and political questions often take on the guise of religious problems and are fought out using the rhetoric of religion, and so it was in great part with the irreconcilable enmity between the Ottomans and the Safavids. Religious opinions were issued by the sheikh ul-Islam against the Safavids to rally emotional support behind and to justify the act of war against another Muslim state. A religious opinion was written in the form of a question and answer. The following example is typical.

If the schismatics of Persia (May God abandon them) who live in the land of Persia under the rule of the sons of Shah Ismail consider as disbelievers those who recognize Abu-Bakr, 'Umar, and 'Uthmān as rightful caliphs, and they themselves hold the rest after Ali as possessors of nobility (May God's approbation be upon them) . . . and if they consider them [the first three caliphs] as apostates and backbiters and openly curse and vilify them while considering themselves devout and believe that the killing of Muslims who are the people of the Sunnah is canonically lawful . . . the place where these cursers and believers of such things live, is it the Abode of War?

Obviously, such invective would permit only an affirmative response: "Yes, it is the Abode of War and they can be considered as apostates."

Campaigning in Persia was difficult for the Ottoman army, even with religious justification. The journey from Istanbul to Persia took months. The route was hazardous and many died along the way. Ottoman organizational talents were stretched to the limit to assure the army of adequate supplies at strategic locations, and the inevitably missed connections caused much hardship. In Persia itself the Ottomans met with further hardship because the shah's forces employed scorched-earth techniques as they retreated. Distance, weather conditions, and logistical factors, plus the need for timariots to return to their own provinces and perform their local administrative duties, made the campaigning season short, and military success depended on taking objectives quickly. In addition, the janissaries proved recalcitrant so far from home. In 1514 they had forced Selim I to abandon any notion of wintering in Tabriz, and under Suleiman they were equally unmanageable. Moreover, cities and towns taken during a campaign would revert to Safavid control as soon as the Ottoman army withdrew. Thus, Suleiman's Persian campaigns during the periods 1533–1535 and 1548–1549 had brought the Ottomans control of important trade routes but had also demonstrated that eastern expansion had its limits.

The peace of Amasya in 1555 stabilized the eastern frontier at a time when the Ottomans wished to become heavily engaged elsewhere. Persian affairs demanded the attention of the Ottomans again, however, when a dynastic struggle threatened the Safavids with internal collapse after the death of Shah Tamasp I in 1576. The crisis stemmed from competition for control of the government between the two dominant factions within the Safavid state. One was the Turcoman tribes, the original supporters of Shah Ismail in the organization of the state at the beginning of the sixteenth century, and the other, the newer military and court leaders who came largely from the Caucasus. Ismail II, the candidate of the Turcoman faction, assumed the throne in 1576. His two-year reign was one of incredible violence, in which he killed practically all the possible rival candidates for the throne and many of the preeminent figures of state. Ismail also sought to foment a religious revolt against the Ottomans in Anatolia, but that plan failed. His religious policy in Shirvan, whose inhabitants were Sunnis (Orthodox Muslims), produced an uprising against the Shi'ite governor and appeals to Istanbul for aid.

The Ottomans, considering that the Persian situation was advantageous and presented possibilities for renewed expansion, entered into a series of eastern campaigns that engaged their attention until 1639. Ottoman military objectives and methods underwent significant change in this period. They now sought to effect a permanent occupation of the lands between the Black and Caspian seas and to accomplish this occupation through the conquest and fortification of strategic strongholds. In this manner they hoped to render their eastern frontier secure, impose religious peace over the area, and bring under Ottoman control the rich silk-producing areas along the Caspian Sea. During this time the Ottomans also engaged in further conflict with the Hapsburgs on the European land frontier, thus reverting to the earlier pattern of counterbalancing eastern and western campaigns.

From 1578 to 1590 the Ottomans were mainly concerned with the Caucasus. Valuable assistance from the khan of the Crimea helped to keep the important Caspian Sea port of Derbend in Ottoman hands. In 1579 the city of Kars was converted into an Ottoman fortress and thereafter served as the new base of operations as the Ottomans pressed eastward. Further south the Ottomans launched another arm of their pincer movement. In 1586 Baghdad, Mosul, and the whole of Mesopotamia were annexed to the Ottoman state. Faced with a deteriorating military situation, Shah Abbas I, the new ruler of Persia, sought a peace settlement. A costly peace was arranged in 1590 that left the Ottomans in control of Tabriz as well as other crucial areas.

CONFLICT IN
THE WEST

With the situation in the east temporarily at a standstill, the Ottomans were again free to do battle in the west. Ghazis continued to be active in the border zone between the Ottoman and Hapsburg empires despite the formal state of peace that had existed since 1568. The ghazis staged major raids in 1591 and 1592 but not until June 1593 did the Ottomans resolve upon a total offensive against Hungary. There, as in Persia, the Ottomans engaged in a long, arduous conflict that sapped their strength. During this thirteen-year struggle, known as the Long War, the Ottomans faced a changed situation. The Christians were now better armed and better trained than in earlier conflicts. The Hapsburgs had created a defensive barrier in the Croatian border zone by granting special privileges to anti-Ottoman refugees, who evolved their own methods of combating the Ottomans. This policy enabled the Hapsburgs to offer a stiffer resistance. The Hapsburgs had also strengthened key strongholds. On their part, the Ottomans were forced to rely more upon their own fortresses as well. Thus, the previously fluid border between Christianity and Islam was fast becoming a stabilized line of fortresses protected by outlying smaller defense works. During the course of the war fortresses changed hands many times, and revolts against Ottoman suzerainty in Walachia, Moldavia, and Transylvania lost impetus. The Hungarians struggled to reassert their claims to these areas, but without success. Finally both the Ottomans and the Hapsburgs grew weary of the conflict and negotiated for peace. The sultan was negotiating not as a victor but as an equally debilitated adversary. He had to grant important concessions: The sultan accepted the Hapsburg emperor as an equal and agreed to accept 200,000 gulden instead of tribute from the Hapsburgs. Ottoman rule was to continue in Hungary. A thirteen-year struggle thus ended in a stalemate in November 1606 on the middle Danube. Even that stalemate was achieved at enormous cost in men and materiel and imposed a severe strain on the imperial Ottoman treasury. Conquest, which had been the Ottoman birthright over the centuries, was now purchased at a rapidly increasing price, if at all.

BACK TO
THE EAST

Peace with the Hapsburgs, costly as it was, was a necessity for the Ottomans, who were again faced with a growing menace on their eastern frontier from a reinvigorated Persia led by Shah Abbas II. He had reorganized his military forces and royal household. In 1603 he was ready to battle the Ottomans. Moving to the offensive, Abbas retook Tabriz in 1603. The Ottomans were unable to halt Abbas' advance, because they were preoccupied with the campaigns on the Danube and with rebellions in their own provinces. When peace with the Hapsburgs enabled the Ottomans to take the field against Abbas, much had already been lost in the Caucasus, and the seemingly invincible Kars had fallen to the reforming shah's armies. The indigenous Shi'ite population of the area had never accepted the Sunnite Ottoman rule, despite the fact that they shared a common language. In addition to religious differences, the inhabitants resented the introduction of the Ottoman financial and administrative institutions, including the timar system and its associated tax structure. The Ottomans were forced to fight in this hostile territory, far from their supply bases and under the most adverse conditions. They lost heart for battle, and the death of Sultan Ahmed I in 1617 and the subsequent defeat of an Ottoman force near Tabriz the following year compelled them to seek a peace. In September 1618 this second episode in the long Ottoman-Persian encounter, which had begun in 1517, was brought to an end. A treaty was signed, based on the 1555 Treaty of Amasya, and the Ottomans were back where they had been when Suleiman had ended his campaign against the Safavids. More than half a century of conflict brought the Ottomans only internal unrest and severe strain on their resources. In 1607 the Ottomans had negotiated a treaty with the Hapsburgs that represented a thinly disguised defeat; now in 1618 they were forced to accept a similar agreement with the Persians. Their position was steadily weakening.

The reality of their waning strength, however, was not so obvious to the Ottomans themselves. They were not yet aware that the military and economic tide was turning inexorably toward Europe. They still believed that the setbacks in Hungary and Persia were only temporary. Self-confidence and extraordinary recuperative powers enabled them in a short time to put another army in the field against Abbas. In 1623 Abbas swept the Ottomans out of Baghdad and the rest of Mesopotamia, but in the same year Murad IV came to the throne and began a campaign that temporarily restored the empire to health. This sultan, the most energetic since Suleiman, was a throwback to the earlier warrior-sultans who had campaigned in person at the head of their armies. Throwing himself into matters of state, he succeeded in reasserting central authority. With discipline restored in the empire, he marched into the Caucasus at the head of a powerful army and in 1635 retook the city of Erivan. Baghdad also fell, and in 1639 a treaty was signed between the Ottomans and the Safavids that left Baghdad and Kars in Ottoman hands in return for an Ottoman evacuation of Azerbaijan.

Murad IV died in 1640, and thereafter a severe internal crisis, which had been in the making since the reign of Mohammed III, reached fruition. This crisis revolved around the succession to the sultanate. The Ottoman practice had always been for son to succeed father on the throne and for brothers of the new sultan to be executed in an attempt to short circuit palace intrigue. One male member of the family, however, was left alive in case the sultan died without heirs. When Sultan Mohammed III died in 1603 leaving no sons, he was succeeded by his brother Ahmed I, whose life had wisely been spared. Another brother, Mustafa, had also been permitted to live because he was retarded. When Ahmed I died before his sons had reached maturity, his brother Mustafa was of necessity brought to the throne; but his incompetence was so blatant that he was removed after a reign of one hundred days and replaced by Osman II, the fourteen-year-old son of Ahmed I. Four years later Osman was assassinated, and his brother Murad IV ascended the throne at the age of eleven. Murad was able to a great extent to repair the confusion that had come about during the two previous reigns, but when he died the succession to the sultanate developed into a real crisis.

All of Murad's sons were dead. He was therefore succeeded by his remaining brother, Ibrahim, who was psychologically unequal to his high office. The reason for his inability to cope may have been a practice that also dated back to the time of Mohammed III. Before Mohammed's reign the princes of the dynasty had always been sent out to the provinces to gain governmental experience. Mohammed, however, discontinued this practice, and thereafter the princes were kept shut up in special chambers of the palace, called the *kafes*, or "cage," where they lived in fear of their lives. When Ibrahim came to the throne, therefore, he had had no experience in government and had been debilitated by living in constant fear as well as by other factors. It is not surprising that he was not up to ruling the empire. A cabal in the palace convinced his mother, Kösem Sultan (the Queen Mother, or *valide*), that he would have to be deposed. In August 1648 Ibrahim

74

was replaced by his young son Mohammed IV (1648–1687) and subsequently murdered. After the accession of Mohammed IV brothers were no longer put to death, but remained in the *kafes*, and the eldest living male member of the ruling family would then assume the throne. Seniority thus replaced the concept of the will of God exercising itself through one of several sons besting his brothers for the throne, often in open conflict.

SULTANATE OF THE WOMEN

Mohammed IV was only seven years old at the time of his accession, a situation lending itself to palace intrigue. His mother, Turhan, in association with leading figures in the state, sought to control the government. Her archrival, Kösem, mother of Ibrahim, and grandmother of Mohammed IV, also had her supporters among the elite. Kösem plotted with the janissary leaders to eliminate her competitor and place Mohammed's brother, Suleiman, on the throne, but, before she could bring her plan to fruition, she was murdered by Turhan's supporters. Turhan then held complete sway in Istanbul as the power behind the throne. This fascinating period in Ottoman history, in which strong-willed women wielded power, is known as "The Sultanate of the Women."

Turhan encouraged her son's interest in hunting while she herself managed the affairs of the state. She was assisted by a succession of grand viziers, each of whom owed his office and his subsequent disgrace to the fierce infighting among competing palace pressure groups. None of these viziers could find the remedy for the empire's myriad ailments. Tenure in that high position grew insecure, and several grand viziers were executed in office. Leadership failed to materialize, and self-interest dominated the temper of the times. Anatolia was aflame with insurrection, the treasury was chronically empty, and public security on the roads was almost nonexistent.

Even those dangers, however, paled before an immediate and direct threat posed to the empire's very existence. The Venetians and the Ottomans were mortal enemies and had been clawing at each other again since 1643. The bone of contention this time was the island of Crete, Venice's last significant possession in the Mediterranean. The challenge came at a bad moment, for the Ottomans' naval affairs were in disarray. The disorder was so bad that in May 1656 a man without naval experience was appointed grand admiral of the fleet. The new admiral's main distinction was his wealth, and those who appointed him hoped that he would outfit the much-needed fleet at his own expense. However, he proved to be intelligent as well as wealthy and quickly extricated himself from his predicament by purchasing the governorship of Egypt. He was succeeded by Kenan Pasha, a man equally without sea experience, but who was the *valide's* son-in-law, and as such would receive the support of the palace.

Things went badly for Kenan Pasha right from the start. In mid-June of 1656 he led a large but poorly equipped and undermanned fleet out of Istanbul and down the narrow straits. At the Dardanelles the Venetian fleet inflicted upon him the worst naval defeat since Lepanto, and he fled the scene in disgrace. Another pasha, who was on his way with a large retinue to take up a new post as governor of Silistre on the Danube, heard of the debacle at the straits and marched his men down the Gallipoli peninsula to defend the fortress of Kilid Bahr at its tip. He succeeded in repulsing several Venetian landing parties there, thus averting a total calamity.

News of the defeat suffered by Kenan Pasha and his fleet spread fear throughout Istanbul. When the Venetians captured Lemnos and Tenedos, islands that enabled them to blockade the Dardanelles effectively, that fear turned into panic. Prices of commodities rose in the face of anticipated shortages and prices of property fell drastically as many prepared to sell out and flee to the safety of Anatolia. The government, seeking a scapegoat for the disastrous turn of events, turned its wrath upon Mesud Efendi, the sheikh ul-Islam, who was dismissed from office, banished to Anatolia, and shortly thereafter assassinated in Bursa. Still the situation remained perilous: the grand vizier hesitated to take resolute action, and Mohammed IV continued to pursue his passion for hunting. Many palace politicians realized that the empire needed a grand vizier of courage and

vision. The empire had not had an accomplished vizier
since the death of Mohammed Sokollu in 1579. Several
imperial divan meetings were held to uncover such a man,
and the palace was absorbed in feverish backstair politick-
ing. Finally Turhan, without whose assent no changes
could be effected, was convinced to support the nomination
of Mohammed Kuprili as grand vizier, and on September
15, 1656, the incumbent was dismissed and the seals of
office proffered to Kuprili.

THE
KUPRILI ERA
At first nothing about Mohammed Kuprili hinted that this
octogenarian would restore the Ottoman fortunes and become the founder of the empire's most illustrious family
after the dynasty itself. He was born in the 1570s, of an
obscure and totally undistinguished family, probably in
Albania. At an early age he was apprenticed to the imperial
palace in Istanbul, where he served in the candy kitchen,
later moving up to cook. His palace career was in no way
spectacular, and in a *chikma* he passed out of the palace
to take up a timar in Anatolia. He did, however, gain the
patronage of Husrev Aga, who held several important
palace positions, including cloak-bearer and arms-bearer to
the sultan and eventually grand vizier. Kuprili served Husrev in a variety of posts, and when Husrev died, after having been banished by Murad IV, Kuprili, then in his
mid-fifties, found himself without a patron. Rebounding
from that misfortune, he attached himself to a patron even
more powerful, Murad IV's last and by far most talented
grand vizier. Kuprili served under the grand vizier as the
grand equerry.

At about the age of sixty Kuprili received the first of a
number of posts that gave him firsthand knowledge of the
deteriorating situation in the provinces and resulted in his
receiving the rank of vizier. He returned to Istanbul, but
soon quarreled with the grand vizier, was banished to the
provinces, and then exiled to his home base in Anatolia.
He returned to Istanbul in 1656 in the retinue of Grand
Vizier Boynuyarali Mohammed Pasha. In September of
that year he replaced Boynuyarali as grand vizier.

Prior to his elevation to the grand vizierate Mohammed

Kuprili's career was long, but undistinguished. No betting man would have given him much chance to survive, let alone to succeed in any effort to reinvigorate the state. Such a view, however, looks only at the externals. In fact, Kuprili had much in his favor. His years of experience in the retinues of leading officials, including several grand viziers, had served as a training ground. He knew at first hand the ills that beset the state, and years of banishment and withdrawal from active service had given him the leisure to reflect upon possible remedies. When the call came it did not find him unprepared. Kuprili's long experience had also taught him wisdom: He was mindful of the insecurity of his position and cognizant of the influence exercised in state affairs by palace cliques. Kuprili presented to Turhan the terms under which he would accept the seals of office, terms designed to protect himself and enhance his power. His conditions were four: the sultan would not accept or issue commands on the basis of any written communication that did not emanate from Kuprili himself; no vizier or other man of state would act independently of the grand vizier; the grand vizier would give appointments with no interference, no matter how high or low the office; and the sultan would pay no attention to calumnies directed against the grand vizier. Turhan accepted Kuprili's conditions, and Mohammed, in order to preserve the appearance that he and not his mother was the supreme authority, confirmed that acceptance in a public audience. With this assurance of support, Mohammed Kuprili set about to restore the state.

At the heart of Kuprili's plan was the simple notion that there must be an end to corruption and graft in the empire. He acted with a fine balance of finesse and force. He removed corrupt officials from office, regardless of the loftiness of their positions: the sheikh ul-Islam, the grand admiral of the fleet, and the commander of the janissaries were among those ousted. His reach even extended into the palace, where the chief black eunuch, who was an adviser to the *valide* and a notorious meddler in state affairs, was banished to Egypt. He also believed that innovations, condemned by Islamic religious law and popular sentiment alike, which had developed over the years, were the cause for internal ills. His aim was to return the state to the ways of Suleiman the Magnificent, who is known in Ottoman history as the lawgiver. By restoring institutions to the pristine glory they had known at their height in the sixteenth century and by respecting and enforcing the body of Ottoman law codified under Suleiman, the empire could be returned to its past glory. Once Kuprili had brought the public officials into line, he turned his attention to the empire's internal and external foes. Rebellion was put down at home, and the war against Venice was pressed on with determination.

Simple as his program was, it was remarkably successful. The rebels in Anatolia were brought to heel. The principal revolt, led by Abaza Hasan Pasha in the years 1657 and 1658, was particularly dangerous because it not only involved leading governmental figures, but also elicited the support of the people through promises of social and economic reform. Mohammed Kuprili threw a huge force against the troublesome malcontents, and after a bloody combat they were defeated. In the traditional manner, many heads, including that of Abaza Hasan Pasha, were cut off and sent to the capital to be displayed there as a warning to others who might contemplate a challenge to the state's authority.

Kuprili had come to power because of the immediate danger posed to Istanbul by the Venetian occupation of Lemnos and Tenedos. He therefore turned his attention to those thorns as soon as it became feasible. He personally supervised the preparation of a fleet, which was then despatched to retake the islands. Tenedos fell in August 1657 and Lemnos in November. The pressure on the capital was relieved. With his navy functioning again, Kuprili found it possible to prosecute the campaign for Crete with great vigor.

Kuprili had based his program of recovery on the model of Suleiman. It was not unreasonable, therefore, that he should soon try to emulate Suleiman on the battlefield in Central Europe. Transylvania was the key to Ottoman expansionist policy in Central Europe, for it was the bridge to both Hungary and Poland. During the period of debility that preceded the Kuprili regime, Ottoman authority in Transylvania had all but disappeared. George II Rakoczy, prince of Transylvania, led the movement to rid his land of the Ottomans. He also harbored ambitions to reign over Poland, which, in cooperation with Sweden, he invaded in 1655. Kuprili decided to move against Rakoczy. He called for the unruly vassal's deposition and imposed a rival candidate as prince. When Rakoczy drove the Ottoman figurehead out of Transylvania, Kuprili led a full-scale campaign against him with the participation of the Crimean Tartars. Rakoczy's forces were no match for the Ottomans, and Rakoczy himself died of wounds received in battle. The new prince agreed to an increase in the tribute sent to the sultan and the garrisoning of key positions by Ottoman troops. Mohammed Kuprili, however, did not live to see the restoration of complete quiet in Transylvania.

In October 1661, at the height of his prestige and influence, Mohammed Kuprili died. He had accomplished his mission to restore the fortunes of the state. Upon his own recommendation the grand vizierate passed to his son Fazil Ahmed Kuprili, a comparative youngster of twenty-six. Ahmed Kuprili's elevation to the grand vizierate was not merely a case of nepotism. His appointment ensured the continuity of Kuprili's program. Furthermore, he was in his own right an experienced, capable, and intelligent administrator and military commander. Where his father had ruled with an iron hand, Ahmed was more compassionate, but then his father's successes had made a more relaxed atmosphere possible.

Under Ahmed Kuprili the Ottomans began to reassert themselves in Hungary. In July 1664 a treaty was arranged between the Hapsburgs and Ottomans, but military activity continued pending ratification. The Ottomans crossed the Raab River and clashed with the Hapsburg army at St. Gotthard. The Hapsburgs drove the Ottomans back across the river, with both sides suffering great losses, but they did not pursue the retreating Ottomans. When the Hapsburgs ratified the Treaty of Vasvar the campaign came to an end. Only northern and western Hungary remained under Hapsburg control. Ahmed Kuprili's prestige as a commander, which had not been diminished by the defeat at St. Gotthard, rose even more when the Ottomans finally completed their conquest of Crete in 1669. Ottoman forces were also successful in Poland, where the fortresses of Khotin and Kamenets Podolski on the Dnieper River fell to them. Now the Ottoman army ranged as far as Lwow. Both those strongholds, along with the whole of Podolia, remained in Ottoman hands by the peace treaty of 1676. This advance proved to be the deepest penetration the Ottomans would make to the north and west of the Black Sea. Soon after the conclusion of the treaty, Ahmed Kuprili died.

SECOND SIEGE OF VIENNA
European observers of the Ottoman scene were convinced that Mohammed Kuprili and his son Ahmed had not only restored the empire to health, but that they had also placed new power and glory within its grasp. Fear of the Turks, a phobia that had swept Europe in the sixteenth century, was rampant again. Directing the Ottoman enterprise was Kara Mustafa Pasha, the brother-in-law of Ahmed Kuprili. Kara Mustafa was well educated, experienced in government, and a firm adherent to the Kuprili formula of domestic peace, sound administration, and vigorous foreign policy. Conquest was uppermost in his mind. He was to launch the empire upon the ultimate test of whether the restoration achieved by the Kuprilis was permanent or temporary. Kara Mustafa's project was a full-scale attack upon the city of Vienna, the prize that had just managed to elude Suleiman in 1529. Such a conquest would inscribe his name among the outstanding ghazis of Islamic history. In 1692 the Treaty of Vasvar, which had been contracted with the Hapsburgs in 1662, came up for renewal. Kara Mustafa Pasha took an intractable position in the negotiations. In October, after negotiations inevitably broke down, Kara Mustafa Pasha began to gather his forces. By the end of March 1683 all was ready for departure. With Sultan Mohammed IV in the van of the army, the Ottomans reached Belgrade early in May. On May 13 Kara Mustafa was officially given command, and a week later, strengthened by reinforcements, he headed northward.

Estimates of the Ottoman strength vary from 200,000 to 500,000 men, although the effective fighting force has been put at 90,000. Kara Mustafa Pasha and his huge army appeared before the gates of the Hapsburg imperial city on July 14, 1683. In conformity with Islamic law he invited the city to surrender and accept Islam—or else let the sword decide. He received no answer; the Ottomans settled down to gain the sword's decision. European relief of the city was slow in coming. Brandenburg and Saxony contributed some assistance, but Louis XIV of France, who intended to use the discomfiture of the Hapsburgs to further his own anti-Hapsburg cause, delayed. Sobieski of Poland, however, leading an allied force of some 20,000, reached the beleaguered city and provided much-needed strength to resist the siege. The Hapsburgs' possession of heavy artillery and the Ottomans' lack of it finally turned the tide of battle against Kara Mustafa Pasha. The decisive battle was fought on September 12, 1683, when an allied Christian force launched an all-out attack upon the Ottomans and drove them from their encampment. Casualties were high on both sides, and the Christians captured great quantities of booty, lovely examples of which can still be seen in leading European museums. Kara Mustafa Pasha was compelled to withdraw all the way to Belgrade before he could regroup his forces. He planned to winter in Belgrade and then launch a counteroffensive in the spring, but powerful enemies in Istanbul succeeded in undermining his position with the sultan. On December 25, 1683, he was strangled in Belgrade, with the sultan's consent.

AFTERMATH OF 1683

Kara Mustafa Pasha's execution deprived the Ottomans of their most able military mind. It also dampened initiative by setting the price of failure at the forfeiture of one's life, a price that his less-capable successors were unwilling to pay. Sultan Mohammed IV sought to place the blame for the failure at Vienna solely upon the dead grand vizier's audacity, contending that he had been uninformed as to Kara Mustafa Pasha's real goal and would not have sanctioned such a try for Vienna.

In the spring of 1684 a Holy League was formed among

the Austrian Hapsburgs, Poland, and Venice to press their advantage against the Ottomans. Venice attacked along the Dalmatian coast and in Bosnia, Austria along the middle Danube, and Poland along the Black Sea coast. The West tried again to interest the Safavids in opening a second front against the Ottomans, but to no avail. Russia assisted the allies in 1687 with a strike against the Crimean Tartars. Ottoman losses were mounting, especially in Greece. Public indignation grew at the sultan's unwillingness to abandon his favorite sport of hunting and devote himself to the conduct of state business. The military despaired of the sultan's leadership, and in November 1687 they revolted and brought his brother Suleiman II (1687–1691) to the throne. He was followed in swift succession by Ahmed II (1691–1695) and then by Mustafa II (1695–1703). The empire appeared to be foundering on the rocks of internal discord and external defeat.

Events in Europe—the English Revolution of 1688 and 1689, which involved the Hapsburgs against Louis XIV, and the death of Pope Innocent XI in 1689, which deprived the Holy League of its animating force—relieved the pressure against the Ottomans at least temporarily. The Ottoman army was now under the command of Mustafa Kuprili, yet another member of that illustrious family. In 1691 Mustafa led the army in the capture of Belgrade, which the Ottomans had lost in 1688, and from there he was determined to carry the war to the enemy; but at Slankamen he lost his life in a battle against Louis of Baden, and his army was decimated. Thereafter, military matters deteriorated rapidly. The forces of Peter the Great challenged the Ottoman control of the Black Sea. On the seas they carried on hit-and-run tactics against the Venetians, but no decisive actions were fought.

Mustafa II brought about a return to a more aggressive policy. From 1695 to 1696 he launched a counteroffensive against the Austrians, demonstrating more zeal than had his immediate predecessors. Mustafa's efforts were also marked with more success than the Ottomans had known in recent years. This success was due not just to Mustafa's leadership, but also to the fact that the Hapsburgs had been forced to shift their best forces and commanders to Italy, France, and other parts of Europe to meet demands of the war of the Grand Alliance. A change in Hapsburg commanders in 1697 had immediate and far-reaching repercussions for the Ottomans. In that year Frederick Augustus, Elector of Saxony and commander of the Hapsburg forces, was elected King of Poland. He was succeeded as commander by a great military strategist, Eugene of Savoy. On September 4, 1687, Eugene won his first major victory over the Ottomans. At Senta in Hungary he completely mauled the Ottoman army before the very eyes of the sultan, who just managed to escape with his own life. Ottoman losses were great not only in numbers, but in depth as well, with the first, second, and even third levels of command being wiped out.

Another Kuprili emerged as grand vizier during this trying period. He was Hussein Amcazade Kuprili, great-nephew of the first Kuprili. Hussein Pasha realized that with the army seriously handicapped and the empire badly in need of tranquility, he must align himself with those in favor of a peace settlement. Using the good offices of Lord William Paget, the English ambassador at the Porte, he entered into peace negotiations at Karlowitz in Croatia. There the Hapsburgs, Poland, Venice, and Russia bargained with the sultan's representatives. Much time was consumed in formalities that almost wrecked the conference, but finally peace was arranged on the basis of uti possidetis (a legal term meaning that each side would keep the territories in their actual control at the time). Russia arranged a truce and then withdrew from the negotiations because Peter the Great still had ambitions in the Crimea. On January 26, 1699, the Treaty of Karlowitz was signed, calling for Ottoman evacuation of Transylvania and Hungary everywhere except in the Banat of Temsevar. Venice retained possession of the Morea in Greece, and Poland regained Podolia. Belgrade remained in Ottoman control, small consolation for the bitter pill the Ottoman people would have to swallow. For the first time territory that had long been Muslim would pass permanently under Christian control. Slowly but perceptibly, the curtain was descending on the story of the Turkification of the Balkans that had begun in the early fourteenth century. Tenacity of spirit, however, was always a distinguishing Ottoman characteristic. In the second half of the nineteenth century, more than a hundred and seventy-five years after Karlowitz, William Gladstone would bellow for a movement to drive the Turks "bag and baggage" out of Europe.

Chapter 4

Ottoman Consciousness

Soul-searching is often a by-product of disaster, and the disasters of the seventeenth century produced much soul-searching among the Ottomans. Statesmen, historians, men of letters, and palace politicians all sought to identify the malaise that had attacked the Ottoman system and brought it so low. They wrote books directed at their fellow Ottomans, drew up memoranda to guide men in authority, and composed mirrors for princes to give rulers insight into the pressing problems of the day. All these genres had roots in the literary heritage of the High Islamic tradition. The authors were intelligent, concerned, and well meaning. They were devoted to their religion, their state, and their Ottoman way of life. In their writings they hoped to identify the causes of the reversal in Ottoman fortunes and to find remedies to purge their society of its festering cankers. They were good Muslim products of the traditions of High Islam that they were subjecting to scrutiny, and, since they wrote within the framework of that tradition, it is not surprising to find a good deal of similarity in their analyses and in the literary metaphors with which they illuminated their discussions.

The views of these commentators upon Ottoman decline were expressed in the phraseology of Near Eastern statecraft and were predicated upon the "circle of equity," a simple but all-encompassing formulation that embodied the ethical, political, and social values of the Ottoman class. In the manner of its employment, this notion resembles the concept of the "state of nature" expounded by Rousseau and used by European political philosophers. The circle of equity is designed to show the circular relationships among the various classes of the society and their functions in a well-run state.

1. There can be no royal authority without the military.
2. There can be no military without wealth.
3. The *reaya* produce the wealth.
4. The sultan keeps the *reaya* by making justice reign.
5. Justice requires harmony in the world.
6. The world is a garden, its walls are the state.
7. The state's prop is the religious law.
8. There is no support for the religious law without
   royal authority.

These statements were usually written around the circumference of a circle, showing how the eighth statement led directly back to the first. The basis of this political reasoning was the proposition that the state rested upon the fundamental division between the *askeri* and *reaya* classes. The *reaya* paid the taxes that support the military class; *reaya* prosperity depended upon justice; and the sultan's function was to see that justice reigned. Ottoman law was based upon the religious law of Islam and the administrative regulations embodied in the decrees issued by the sultan.

Sari Mehmed Pasha, in his early eighteenth-century work *The Book of Counsel for Vezirs and Governors*, echoed the established position of his fellow Ottomans on this issue.

It is necessary to avoid carefully the introduction of the *reaya* into the *askeri* class. . . . For if the entrance of the *reaya* into the *askeri* class becomes necessary, the *reaya* are diminished and the way is paved for a diminution in treasury receipts. Through these means the structure of the Sublime State is corrupted. The treasury exists through the abundance of the *reaya*. . . . The state exists through them and the revenues collected from them.

In the simplest terms, this view held that in Ottoman society everyone had his place. It was the sultan's function to keep everyone in his place, and the sultan who did this was a just sultan who deserved to be obeyed. Seventeenth-century Ottomans were well aware that the equilibrium so essential to Islamic society had been disturbed and that therein lay the root of Ottoman difficulties. If they could discover the sources of disequilibrium, remove them, and return the state to what it had been under Suleiman the Magnificent, equilibrium would be restored. The examination started seriously with a few writers in the late sixteenth century and continued during the seventeenth century. Throughout this time the writers were agreed that the fundamental factors in the state's debility were a serious decline in the sultan's authority, a breakdown in the timar and *devshirme* systems that resulted in the line between the *askeri* and the *reaya* being blurred, and a tendency for people to forsake their places. These factors, it was agreed, had far-reaching ramifications throughout the state's political and social structure.

DISRUPTION
IN THE TIMAR
SYSTEM

Just as the ideas that formed the circle of equity were interrelated, so, too, were the factors involved in the debility of the state. A good starting point for an analysis of the infirmity afflicting Ottoman society is the breakdown of the timar system. The system was one of the institutions most responsible for the state's early and continued military success and for its sound internal administration. Commencing in the last years of the sixteenth century the timar system no longer functioned at anywhere near its former level of efficiency. At that time inflation began to affect the Ottoman domains, and the financial position of the timar-holders began to erode. Timar incomes were fixed, and the government was in no position to increase their value and thereby close the inflationary gap. Squeezed between the millstones of set stipends and rising prices, many timar-holders could no longer afford to go on campaign. Their grants were then revoked. Others were forced simply to abandon their holdings. Disgruntled, they fled to the cities or swelled the growing ranks of bandit groups that were pillaging the countryside. Revoked and abandoned timars fell into the hands of leading janissaries, influential slaves of the Porte, and palace favorites. Some *reaya* even acquired timars illegally, through bribery. In the mid-seventeenth century several leading janissary officers, including ex-commanders of the janissary corps, somehow managed appointments as chief financial officer of the empire, under whose control were the bureaus that substantiated title to timars and issued the appropriate documents to timar-holders. This office had been held by officials trained in the bureaucracy. For a janissary commander to assume the post was a flagrant example of the disruption of harmony and was no doubt related to the tendency for timars to be awarded to people outside the feudal cavalry body. Corruption at the top was constantly railed against by Ottoman writers, and it bore out the truth embodied in the Turkish proverb, "the fish begins to stink at the head."

As military strength weakened and wealth diminished, justice also declined. The new timar-holders oppressed and exploited the *reaya*, extorting as much as they could in the form of higher taxes and new levies, while shirking the required military service. As a result the feudal cavalry was greatly diminished in size and fighting efficiency, the *reaya* were ground down in misery, the state treasury began to show mounting deficits, public security in the provinces degenerated, and men of non-*askeri* origins entered the military class in increasing numbers.

EXPANSION OF
THE JANISSARY
CORPS

With the deterioration of the feudal cavalry, the military needs of the empire had to be met by other means. Those means were primarily a dramatic increase in the number of the janissary corps and the *Sipahis* of the Porte. In 1527 the number of janissaries stood at close to 8,000;

by 1609 the number had mounted to almost 38,000, nearly a fivefold increase in less than a century. A similar increase took place among the *Sipahis* of the Porte. Their strength rose from 5,000 to almost 21,000 in the same years. Although there is no way to be certain, it would appear that most of the increase in both those organizations stemmed from the enrollment of the sons of janissaries and *Sipahis* of the Porte. Some of the *reaya* also found their way into the military class.

Loud complaints were raised against the entrance of the *reaya* into the military class, for thereby they escaped their tax obligations and undermined the circle of equity. Opposition to the enrollment of janissary sons and the sons of members of other corps was more muted and in many quarters was looked upon as a virtue. Their enrollment into the janissaries and other corps was a natural outgrowth of the process set in motion by Selim I and his successor Suleiman the Magnificent, both of whom relaxed the regulations that prohibited the janissaries from marrying. Those janissaries who married then pressured the government into condoning the enrollment of their sons into the corps. Other slaves of the Porte followed.

The problems arising from the enrollment of janissary sons into the corps were more subtle and less immediately discernible than those connected with the upward mobility of *reaya* into the military class. The *ghulam* system, of which the janissary corps was an integral part, had as its rationale the development of a body of men devoted solely to the sultan's service. When other considerations entered into the lives of the janissaries, such as concern for their own families, their dedication to the sultan's cause began to wane. Janissaries became less willing to undergo the rigors of extended campaigns into distant lands, and instead sought connections in commerce and trade. Forging links with business leaders, they became closely allied with the economies of Istanbul and the garrison towns in which they were stationed. They grew rich, powerful, and more independent. The unruliness of the janissaries and the enrollment of their sons into the corps took its toll on the training and military performance of the corps. Discipline eroded, and the men became extremely recalcitrant.

As the competence of the janissaries declined, their monetary demands rose. Janissary pay, ceremonially distributed once every three months, fell seriously into arrears early in the seventeenth century when the central treasury began to experience severe financial difficulties. Late payments and payments in debased coinage, which amounted to an enforced cut in salary, led to numerous uprisings, especially in Istanbul. It had also been customary for each sultan to extend a cash bonus to the janissaries upon his accession to the throne. The gift was presented in a ceremony during which the sultan toasted the troops with a glass of sherbet, promising to salute them again in Rome. As the janissaries became a more powerful factor in internal politics and as changes in reign became more frequent, they forced the sultans to increase the size of their accession donations, in what might be considered a cost-of-living adjustment. The monetary demands of the increased numbers of janissaries put mounting pressure on the central treasury which resulted in a heavier hand being applied on the *reaya*, and that in turn produced more trouble in the provinces.

SEKBANS AND CELALIS

Provincial unrest had been a prominent feature of Ottoman life since the 1560s. It was associated in many ways with the military difficulties of the empire and concomitant social and financial problems. These interrelated ills are seen in microcosm in the series of rebellions, known as the *celâlî* revolts, that swept Anatolia in the late sixteenth and early seventeenth centuries.

Some of the origins of the *celâlî* revolts are found in the military measures taken by the Ottomans to cope more effectively with the Hapsburg forces, which had been equipped with firearms. One measure taken was to train segments of the enlarged janissary corps in the use of firearms. Another was the organization of a new body of troops, called *sekbans*, who were armed with muskets and gained a reputation as sharpshooters. They were recruited in the late sixteenth century from among landless peasants, dispossessed timar-holders, and Anatolian nomads. The central government enrolled these sharpshooters in cavalry and infantry units. Their salaries were covered by new sources of funds derived from tax farms created out of vacant timars. Additional *sekbans* were recruited by the provincial governors, who took them into their own services, as they had done with slaves in earlier centuries. These provincial *sekbans* were contributed to the sultan's army as part of the governor's own military obligation. The provincial governors were empowered to levy a special tax on the peasants for the maintenance of the *sekbans* under their banners. When the *sekbans* were sent back to Anatolia at the conclusion of a campaign, however, they received no pay. When these unemployed troops could find no work in Anatolia, they swelled the ranks of rebel gangs who had turned to brigandage, forcibly levying taxes on town and village dwellers, ravaging the countryside, and creating general havoc.

Between 1595 and 1610 these brigands terrorized Anatolia. The sultan's authority was reduced to nothing. Real power was in the hands of the brigand leaders. They were able to put as many as 20,000 men into the field against the forces of the central government. Such a situation could not be allowed to continue. The sultan sent his most dependable forces against the brigands and subdued them between 1607 and 1610.

Janissaries and *Sipahis* of the Porte were then stationed in the main towns to continue the pacification of Anatolia. There they followed the same patterns they had developed in Istanbul. They established ties with the leading elements in the local society, engaged in trade and commerce, married into the influential families, and eventually dominated the local scene. When the central government's hold over the provinces grew weaker and weaker in the eighteenth and nineteenth centuries, these new figures developed into the leaders, known as notables (*ayan*), of provincial society.

CAUSES   *Population Growth*   Ottoman writers have attributed the empire's troubles to the dissolution of the circle of equity, and specifically to the erosion of the sultan's authority, the disruption of the timar system, and the

93

demise of the *devshirme*. In reality they were describing symptoms rather than causes. At the root of the problems were several complex causes. One of those causes was a serious population explosion that began in the sixteenth century. Population growth appears to have outstripped the increase in new lands brought under cultivation, creating a large group of landless peasants with very little opportunity for earning a livelihood. They supplied much of the manpower in the *sekban* companies, where they were exposed to combat and the use of firearms. It was only a natural progression for them to use these skills for banditry when they returned to unemployment in Anatolia. This challenge to the sultan's authority did not escape the eyes of Ottoman writers, but the underlying demographic changes were beyond their comprehension.

Inflation   Another cause of the problems was inflation. State income was derived mainly from agricultural revenues and was predicated upon a stable currency. The Ottoman economy was a regulated one in which the marketplace was carefully supervised: weights and measures, prices and profits, imports and exports, guilds and raw materials were all under close government scrutiny. The state acted as a sort of mediator between the manufacturer and the consumer.

The state sought to dominate all trade routes in its area in order to increase customs receipts, deny its enemies access to necessary war material, and ensure itself of a steady flow of vital goods. One of the largest consumers of those goods was the state itself, especially the huge palace complex at Istanbul, and the military. In the interests of the state two price structures prevailed: one was the going market price and the other the government price, which was generally about 25 percent lower.

Ottoman prices remained reasonably stable until 1580, when severe inflation, traced to the influx of cheap Peruvian silver, started to affect the empire. The government resorted to several expedients, including debasing the currency (which only reinforced the inflationary trend), seizing the estates of exiled or executed pashas, raising taxes, and extending tax farming. None of these measures had much effect. Inflation in the Ottoman Empire kept pace with that in Europe, where prices doubled between 1550 and 1600 and by 1650 they were triple those of 1600. Although the capitation tax rose from 25 akchas in Suleiman's reign to 150 akchas in 1596, a sixfold increase, and would double again within another century, the treasury still showed mounting deficits. Extraordinary taxes (*avarid*), levied previously only in emergencies, were converted into an annual tax on all subjects. Assessed at 50 akchas in 1576, it rose to 240 akchas in only a quarter of a century, and still the insatiable treasury growled for more. Just how severe the inflation was can be judged by the fact that in 1564 it took approximately 60 akchas to equal one gold ducat, and by 1648 the exchange rate had doubled. The terrible effects of such rampant inflation were felt both in the provinces and in the central government. The Ottomans were aware of these effects, but short of conjuring up a successful alchemist who could change base metal to gold (alchemy enjoyed a serious revival in this period), the state could find no ready remedy.

End of Conquests Population growth and inflation, compelling as they are as causes for the empire's decay, were only strands in the web of causation. The dominating cause was the fact that by the end of Suleiman the Magnificent's reign the age of Ottoman conquests had come to a grinding halt. The last significant conquests in the West were Cyprus, which fell in 1570, and Crete, taken in 1664. Although there was considerable fighting in Persia, the Ottomans failed to hold any of the territories gained in battle. The Ottoman state was predicated upon, committed to, and organized for conquest. Conquest had provided wealth in the form of new lands for timar grants and for agriculture, more positions for those in bureaucratic and religious careers, additional manpower for the *devshirme*, and booty of infinite variety. Opportunities for financial reward on the expanding frontier had served to drain off potentially turbulent elements in the population. An end to significant and sustained conquest rocked the entire state structure and sent aftershocks through all its institutions. Henceforth, candidates for timars were accommodated mainly through the death of incumbent timar-holders. A crisis in the religious institutions was unavoidable, because the religious schools had overexpanded and enrolled far too many students for the reduced number of jobs that were available. Dissident Muslim seminary students joined the disaffected in the towns and countryside, challenging the authority of the state. The central government's monetary needs had to be met by increasing the tax burden on an already overburdened population, which would in turn feed the fires of unrest. *Devshirme* levies became more difficult to raise from the limited areas already depleted of their young males by earlier enrollments. The frontier was converted from an area in which hopefuls found advancement and fortune into a place where martyrdom was the only reward.

Ottoman Complacency   The shutdown of the land frontier became a serious barrier to the flow of ideas between West and East. The Ottomans had previously been receptive to ideas from the West. For example, they had adopted the use of cannon shortly after they encountered it during early fifteenth-century campaigns in Europe. Now, the Ottomans had ceased to expand, and the Ottoman Islamic culture turned in upon itself in a defensive reaction. The members of the ulema especially maintained the superiority of the Islamic dispensation, heaping scorn upon the outside world. Innovation became a particular object of their wrath, and any deviation from the Sunnah, the established path and mode of Islamic behavior based on the practices of the Prophet and his companions, was to be rooted out. Naima, a broad-minded seventeenth-century Ottoman historian who tried to present the obscurantists in the worst possible light, reports a confrontation between a rigidly orthodox Muslim and a more enlightened Muslim on the subject of innovations. The orthodox Muslim, taking an extreme position, was forced to agree that trousers and underwear were innovations. Indeed, he had no objection to everyone dressing like a bare-bottomed desert Arab.

Notions of Islamic superiority had been further enhanced by the passing of the Islamic millennium. As the Muslim year 1000 A.H. (October 19, 1591–October 7, 1592) approached, there were dire predictions about the world's cataclysmic end. When none of the predictions were fulfilled, the Ottomans took that as a sign of God's approbation and as evidence that the Ottoman Empire had achieved the greatest perfection of any Islamic state. Therefore, there was little the Ottomans could learn from others. This closing of the mind was taking place at the time when crucial scientific and technological changes were taking place in Europe, and as the Ottomans smugly patted themselves on the back the gap between Europe and the empire widened.

Geographical and Logistical Limitations   Ottoman complacency was only one of the factors involved in the loss of their knack for conquest: there were others of perhaps even greater significance. Once the Ottomans had settled upon Constantinople as their capital and made it the premier city in the Islamic world, they had inexorably fixed the limits of their expansion. They were dependent upon oxen, camels, and horses to transport the bulk of their military supplies, and their military organization required the feudal cavalry to disband usually by the end of October. With the standing army increasingly centered in Istanbul, Vienna in the west and Tabriz in the east represented the furthest limits of a season's campaigning. The Ottoman army moved quickly despite the state of the roads it had to traverse, the adverse weather conditions, and the means of transport at its disposal, but it still was not quick enough. In 1529 Suleiman and his huge army left Istanbul on May 10, and did not reach Vienna until September 26, over four months later. This left them at best only about a month in which to capture Vienna before the end of campaigning season. On October 15 the Ottoman retreat began, with Vienna still unconquered. Although the Ottomans did not recognize it at the time, the gates of Vienna represented the high-water mark of their westward expansion. They carried on the struggle for another century and a half and even managed to mount another enormous attack against Vienna in 1683, but the same problems they had experienced in 1529 frustrated them again.

The attractions of Istanbul had captivated Mohammed the Conqueror, and his desire to turn himself into a Caesar and the Ottomans into the heirs of the Byzantine Empire had deflected the Ottomans from their natural nomadic bent. In the past they had relocated their capital periodically to keep pace with the thrust of their advance. As they expanded westward in Anatolia they moved from Eskishehir to Yenishehir, and then to Bursa. From Bursa they shifted their capital to Edirne in order to direct and control the conquest of the Balkans. The shift to Constantinople was irresistible. They would have control of the best natural harbor in the area and would be placed at the point where Asia and Europe meet, the fulcrum of their expansion both to the east and to the west. At that time there was still much to conquer within striking distance of the new imperial center, and they had no sense of any limitation of their conquest. Thus their energies were diverted away from ghazi idealism and channeled into the creation of a great Islamic empire based on the traditions and institutions of High Islam. Istanbul appeared to be the ideal location from which to carry out this scheme.

Events of 1516–1517 denied the Ottomans any other option and committed them to the maintenance of Istanbul as their permanent capital. In that year they took control of the original Islamic heartland, including the two holiest cities in Islam, Mecca and Medina. Once the Ottomans became the champions of Islam on a world-wide front, they could no longer move their capital westward to facilitate further expansion into Europe. Such a move would have situated them too far from Mecca and made it difficult if not impossible to shift their forces eastward in case they had to defend the holy city. It was necessary now to defend the city, not only against non-Muslims such as the Portuguese, but also against the Shi'ite threat posed by the militant Safavids of Persia. The Ottomans, enticed originally by the delights and advantages of Constantinople and now locked in by the dictates of logistics and Sunnite Islamic political strategy, had themselves set the seal on the limits of their expansion. During the reign of Mustafa III (1757–1774) much energy and wealth would be expended on the renovation of Edirne, the previous capital, but that would be done out of antiquarian interests and not for any strategic considerations. By then, of course, it would already be far too late for such a move to make any difference.

The Kuprili program for restoring the state is seen in better perspective against the background of the prevailing intellectual climate. Mohammed Kuprili was completely a product of the Ottoman system. He was dedicated to his faith and his state and to the Ottoman Way. His program was intended to reestablish the sultan's authority throughout the realm and purge the state's institution of the abuses that had caused the empire's decay—the sale of offices, the extortion practiced on the *reaya*, and failure of people to remain in their places. In other words, he meant to restore the balance expressed in the circle of equity.

In 1653 Katib Chelebi, a renowned Ottoman historian, wrote *The Guide to Practice for the Rectification of Defects*, a work intended as a confidential memorandum. In discussing ways to halt the state's headlong rush to disaster, he remarked that only the appearance on the scene of a "man of the sword" could save the Ottomans. Katib Chelebi stated that such a man would have to carry through a series of reforms to reverse the treasury's deficit, limit the excessive growth of the army, and restore the peasantry to prosperity. He was not certain that a new leader would appear, but he encouraged his fellow Ottomans to take heart. The state had known despair before—in its defeat at the hands of Timur and more recently in the *celâli* disorders—but with luck and good management it had overcome these obstacles. In this instance, too, it would win its way back to greatness. Mohammed Kuprili almost fulfilled Katib Chelebi's prediction. Through the single-mindedness of Kuprili and those of his family who succeeded him, the state was restored to health, a severe crisis was weathered, and a modicum of lost greatness was re-captured. The failure of the second siege of Vienna, the series of defeats that followed in its wake, and the humiliating Treaty of Karlowitz, however, produced a new wave of introspection among Ottoman intellectuals.

THE HISTORIAN
NAIMA

Outstanding among the writers who dedicated their talents to exploring the causes of the new crisis and to proposing remedies to their peers was the historian Naima. Naima was born in Aleppo around 1665, the son and grandson of janissary officers who had done well in that important trading city. His family was loyal and dedicated to the sultan. About 1685 Naima went to Istanbul and was enrolled in the halberdier corps of the imperial palace, one of the elite corps in the Outside Service. In the halberdiers he was trained as a secretary. Upon the completion of his training, Naima took up a high-ranking position in the state bureaucracy and attached himself to a number of powerful patrons, including the distinguished Hussein Kuprili, who became grand vizier in 1697. Hussein had the thankless task of making the unpopular Treaty of Karlowitz palatable to the Ottoman public. He had two advantages: his distinguished Kuprili name and the fact that he had advocated continuing the war against the Hapsburgs until it was blatantly obvious that further hostilities would be detrimental to the empire's existence. The one thing Hussein lacked was the eloquence to defend that policy, and for that he enlisted the aid of Naima.

Naima did not disappoint his patron. The Preface to his court chronicle of seventeenth-century Ottoman history, *The Garden of Hussein, Being the Choicest of News of the East and West*, is a deft defense of his patron's policy. In it Naima demonstrates his knowledge of the literature on Islamic statecraft. He draws principally upon the ideas and schema of the Arab historian Ibn Khaldun and Katib Chelebi to convince his fellow Ottomans that Hussein Kuprili's policy was the only sane course.

Naima, in addressing his Muslim audience, shows that Hussein's policy had precedent in the actions of the Prophet Muhammad himself. The incident he discussed is the peace of Hudaybiyah, which was entered into between Muhammad and the Meccans in 627 A.D. He points the moral in the subtitle of the Preface—"written . . . for the purpose of showing how important it is to make armistices with infidel kings . . . so that the domains may be put in order and the population have rest"—by relating a story from the life of the Prophet. In the spring of 627 Muhammad led his followers toward Mecca on what was intended to be an attempt to take the city. They halted at a well in a place called Hudaybiyah. There Muhammad realized his attempt would not be successful and entered into a truce with the Meccans. The subsequent success of Islam attests to the wisdom of the Prophet's action. When not fully prepared to fight, he employed "the means at hand," namely, the conclusion of a truce. In 1699 the Ottoman sultan was faced with a similar situation, and he too had used the best possible "means at hand." A respite had been granted to the state, and it was incumbent upon all loyal Muslim supporters of the Ottoman dynasty to accept the diagnosis of its ills and to participate in the application of the remedies.

THE MEDICAL ANALOGY

Naima's diagnosis employs a familiar Islamic model that identified the state with the human body and the physician with the grand vizier. The state, like the body, goes through the various stages of birth, growth, and decay, and good health depends upon the equilibrium of its four humors. The first part of this analogy, the cyclical theory of history, which harks back to Greek historical notions, was passed on to the Ottomans by Ibn Khaldun (1332–1406). In his *Muqaddimah* Ibn Khaldun maintains that a dynasty, like an individual, grows up, enters into a period of stagnation, and then retrogresses. Each period corresponds to the lifetime of a person, set at some forty years. Ibn Khaldun was a living historical tradition among the Ottomans, who kept his ideas alive until he was "rediscovered" in the twentieth century by Westerners and Arabs alike.

Expanding on the theories of Ibn Khaldun, Naima postulates five stages in the life of a state: the heroic period of its establishment, the period of consolidation under the dynasty and its slave-servants, the period of security and tranquility, the period of contentment and surfeit, and finally, the period of disintegration and dissipation. Under Kara Mustafa Pasha, the unfortunate architect of the second siege of Vienna in 1683, the Ottomans had entered the fourth stage, that of contentment and surfeit. Hussein Kuprili now sought to stimulate recovery from the stupor that had affected the empire.

Naima's diagnosis of the lethargy afflicting the state employs the vocabulary of medical analogy and relies heavily upon the judgment of Katib Chelebi. The four classes are compared to the four humors of the body: the Men of the Sword to phlegm, the Men of the Pen to blood, the Men of Negotiation to yellow bile, and the Men of Husbandry to black bile. Of principal concern in the problem of maintaining equilibrium were phlegm and black bile. Old age in the body is characterized by an excess of phlegm and in the state by an overexpanded military establishment. It is extremely difficult to keep the phlegm (military) under control. The black bile is disturbed through undernourishment. In the early periods the sultans had protected the *reaya* from injustice. In later periods the *reaya* were the victims of oppression and mismanagement. This, in turn, affects one of the central organs of the body, the stomach, which in the state is the treasury. If bile cannot enter the stomach, or wealth cannot enter the treasury, undernourishment results, and the body, or the state, suffers. The function of the physician, or the grand vizier, is to maintain the necessary equilibrium among the humors and classes of society. The medical analogy welds the circle of equity concept to the cyclical theory of history by joining the notions of the body's stages of growth with the healthy equilibrium of the four humors.

Naima, moving from diagnosis to prescription, lays down five principles that could save the state. First, the government should balance income and expenditures, which could best be done by reducing expenditures. Second, the government should pay its stipends and salaries on time, which would quiet outbursts against the government.

102

Third, the government should purge the military of abuses and bring it to full strength in order to resist the foreign enemy and restore tranquility at home. Fourth, the government should administer the provinces justly so as to return the *reaya* to prosperity. Finally, the sultan should be as cheerful as possible. That will make his subjects both love and fear him and thus drive from their minds any thoughts of misconduct. Then, with God's help, the problems will disappear.

EIGHTEENTH-
CENTURY SUCCESS

Naima's recommendations were simple, and they worked. After the respite provided by the Treaty of Karlowitz, the Ottoman army was highly successful. The army defeated the forces of Peter the Great on the banks of the Pruth River in 1711. The most effective Ottoman unit in this encounter was the Crimean Tartars. Armed with the traditional weapons of bows and swords, they cut off so many Russian heads that the grand vizier, who at the beginning of the battle had offered his men a large bounty for every Russian head delivered to his tent, had to reduce the bonus to less than half the amount during the course of the day. Following that historic campaign, the Ottomans retook the Morea from the Venetians in 1715 and defeated the Austrians and the Russians during the period from 1736 to 1739. When peace negotiations with the Austrians were stalled, the Ottoman commander threatened that the road to Vienna was open and his troops knew the way. Belgrade was returned to the Ottomans, and the policy of Hussein Kuprili so ably defended by Naima was more than vindicated.

The Ottoman military success was matched by cultural achievements. The reign of Ahmed III (1703–1730) is remembered as the "Tulip Period," the last flowering of Ottoman artistic refinement. In these years an obsession took hold of the Ottomans for the cultivation of tulips. The tulip became a favorite Ottoman motif in fabrics, tiles, and miniatures. Architecture during the Tulip Period was especially graceful, and this grace is revealed in a number of justly famous summer palaces, fountains, and palatial homes along the Bosporus. This superficial passion for tulips reflected a concern with the externals of life, an attitude which found a similar manifestation in the loveliness of European rococo art and architecture in the eighteenth century. Unfortunately, during the Tulip Period little attention was devoted to the underlying institutional structure of the state.

The eighteenth century saw the intensification of certain trends in Ottoman administration. It became almost imperative that sons follow the careers of their fathers, because the failure to conquer new territory limited career opportunities. The career of the father tended to become the family career. Mobility within career lines was still possible, especially with the help of an influential patron. For example, Mohammed Raghip (born 1699), the son of an undistinguished bureaucrat, followed his father's career, acquired a number of useful patrons, and eventually became grand vizier. Although talent was still rewarded, it never hurt one's career to have a powerful patron.

The curtailment of the *devshirme*, begun in the seventeenth century, produced an interesting development in the eighteenth. "Pasha" was a title indicating that the bearer was a member of the military-administrative career. "Efendi" referred to a bureaucrat or a member of the ulema. The three careers were generally separate and distinct. Rarely did an efendi in the seventeenth century leave the bureaucracy and take up a military-administrative career. Those high-level positions were filled mostly by candidates from the ·*devshirme* and the palace school. With the curtailment and eventual abolition of the *devshirme*, the state was forced to find alternative candidates for those offices, and in the eighteenth century a significant number of men whose careers had formerly been devoted entirely to the bureaucracy shifted into military-administrative positions. They served as governors, and several, like Mohammed Raghip, even rose to occupy the post of grand vizier.

OTTOMAN KNOWLEDGE OF EUROPE

Perhaps the most significant fact about the eighteenth-century Ottomans is that they lived completely within an Islamic environment and frame of reference. They had little personal contact with Europeans. The *reisülküttab* was responsible for the foreign affairs of the empire. His duties brought him into contact with foreign ambassadors and emissaries, but conversations between them were formal and mediated through translators on both sides. Until the Greek Rebellion of the 1820s the Ottoman government relied upon several leading Greek families of the Phanar district in Istanbul for official translators. They were known as the translators of the Porte, and, in reality, they managed the empire's foreign relations. Ambassadors who wished to see the *reisülküttab* arranged appointments through these translators. Of course, this practice gave them considerable power. These Phanariote Greeks identified their interests with those of the Ottomans. When news of the Greek Rebellion reached Istanbul, however, the Ottomans hanged the Greek Patriarch and the chief translator, putting an end to the influence of the Phanariote Greeks at the Porte. After this time Muslims were trained in the European languages.

The overwhelming majority of Ottomans had no first-hand knowledge of Europe. Few of them ever traveled to Europe, and those who did were usually on official business. The Ottoman Empire did not establish permanent diplomatic relations with European powers until 1793. Prior to that time embassies were sent out as necessary, generally to announce the death of a sultan, to exchange treaties, or to transact some other diplomatic business. European literature had a vast body of writing on travel in the Levant, but Ottoman literature had nothing comparable on Europe. In fact, the Ottoman ruling elite knew very little about Europe and were not noticeably interested in learning more. When they thought about Europe at all, it was with a vague, comforting idea that Europe was inferior to their own Islamic world.

Some Ottomans did become more conscious of the existence of Europe and its significance. Katib Chelebi, for example, in writing a work on geography, concluded that Muslim sources were inadequate for information of the Christian lands. He therefore sought information on Christian geography from a renegade French priest who had converted to Islam. Even this limited, secondhand knowledge of Europe put Katib Chelebi far ahead of his fellow Ottomans. The following passage from his book on naval warfare is indicative of both his courage in transcending the narrow confines of his own culture and the superficiality of the information he was able to gather despite all his efforts.

For the man who is in charge of affairs of state, the science of geography is one of the matters of which knowledge is necessary. If he is not familiar with what the entire earth's sphere is like, he should at least know the map of the Ottoman domains and that of the states adjoining it, so that when there is a campaign and military forces have to be sent, he can proceed on the basis of knowledge, and so that the invasion of the enemy's land and also the protection and defense of the frontiers becomes an easier task. Taking counsel with individuals who are ignorant of that science is no satisfactory substitute, not even when such men are of the region. Most locals are entirely unable to sketch the map of their own home region. Sufficient and compelling proof of the necessity for [learning] this science is the fact that the unbelievers, by their application to and their esteem for those branches of learning, have discovered the New World and have overrun the ports of India and the East Indies. Nor is that all. Even such a miserable lot as the Venetians, a people whose ruler has only the rank of duke among the unbeliever kings, and whom those kings call "the fisherman," has actually advanced to the Dardanelles of the Ottoman domains and has set itself to oppose the all-glorious state which rules over east and west.

Katib Chelebi's plea for more awareness of developments in Europe and of their implications for the future of the Ottoman state had little result. The government continued to gather and process information about the political affairs of Europe, but it paid little heed to deeper and more significant developments in the intellectual, scientific, and technological spheres. Cosmopolitan and sophisticated in terms of their own Islamic world and environment, the Ottomans were terribly provincial with respect to the world beyond Islamic frontiers. As long as they remained victorious and the gap between them and the West remained, at worst, narrow, such an attitude was not dangerous or even reprehensible. When Ottoman arms were no longer victorious and Europe began to pull ahead of the Islamic world, however, such a point of view became dangerous and counterproductive.

SUCCESS
BREEDS FAILURE As discussed earlier, the Ottomans' response to their failure to sustain perpetual victory was wholly within the Islamic frame of reference. Familiar symbols, such as the circle of equity and the medical analogy, were used to identify the ills of the state, and an equally familiar solution was called for: restore, purge, and revitalize. All eyes looked backward, measuring their own performance against the ideal—the reign of Suleiman the Magnificent, when the empire was clearly at its height. They had only to discover how things were done then and follow that example. There was no thought of innovation, no willingness to experiment with new institutions. Islam abhors innovation, a position traceable to a saying of the Prophet that "the worst things are those that are novelties, every novelty is an innovation, every innovation is an error, and every error leads to Hell-fire." Once morality was reintroduced into society and strong viziers dispensed harsh punishment to offenders, justice would reign, and the empire would again achieve great victories.

Both Katib Chelebi and Naima, in their own times, had predicted the resurgence of the Ottoman strength, and events proved them right. Twice the requisite breathing spell had indeed enabled the Ottomans to be victorious again. That very success, however, soon bred an ultimate failure that transformed the Ottoman state. After the end of the great struggle against Russia and Austria in 1739, the Ottomans entered upon a long period of peace on their western frontier. Europe became enmeshed in its own affairs, most notably with the Seven Years' War, in which the Ottoman Empire intelligently refused to become involved. The ruling elite, left to its own devices, found life in Istanbul uneventful. The court observed round after round of meaningless ceremonies, and ennui set in. That ennui was dissipated in 1768, when the Ottomans went to war against Russia.

OTTOMAN-
RUSSIAN WAR

The immediate cause of this third major Ottoman-Russian confrontation was the situation in Poland. When Augustus III of Poland died in 1763, the great European powers entered into furious diplomatic maneuverings to elect a new king. Russia and Prussia wanted a king who would not be under the domination of Austria. In 1764 combined pressure from Russia and Prussia brought about the election of Stanislaw Poniatowski by the Polish Diet. France, her own plans frustrated, urged the Ottomans to intervene in Polish affairs. The Poles resisted Poniatowski's efforts to alter their constitution and formed the Confederation of Bar to oppose him. While pursuing forces of the confederation, Ukrainian irregulars burned the city of Balta. The Ottomans held the Russians responsible for that action, and in October 1768 they declared war on Russia. Neither side was prepared for war, and the struggle took on the aspect of conflict between the one-armed and the blind. For four years the war dragged on, interrupted sporadically by attempts to reach a negotiated settlement. Finally peace was arranged at Küchük Kainarja in July 1774.

This peace brought a house of cards down around the heads of the Ottomans. Their self-image as a revitalized, restored empire, fostered by almost three-quarters of a century of renewed success, was shattered. The pharmacology of Islam, as prescribed by Naima and practiced by the Ottoman ruling elite, had brought only the illusion of restored health. It resembled a last rallying before death, rather than a complete cure. The treaty of Küchük Kainarja was the first tremor that shook the Ottomans out of their lethargy and complacency. The realization began to grow that the diagnosis and prescription they had put their faith in was, in the final analysis, made by a physician who had not been allowed to view the patient and who had prescribed only sugared pills. If the empire were to continue to exist, a new understanding of its problems and fresh solutions would have to be found.

SELIM III

That new understanding was slow in developing, but develop it did. Although many clung to the older ways, a

108

new, strong-willed sultan, Selim III (1761–1808), began to initiate the necessary reforms. The Ottomans turned first to the West, seeking to equal its level of military capability. They organized a new army, trained and equipped in the European manner. In 1792 and 1793 the reforming sultan promulgated a series of regulations designed to restructure the state's administration and military organization. His far-reaching program was known as the New Order. Language instruction played a central role in the new Western orientation of the empire. Young Ottomans were trained in French, and permanent diplomatic missions were opened in the main capitals of Europe. Gradually Western ideas would filter into the empire and help transform it in the nineteenth century into a more modern state. Sultan Selim III stood midway between the old traditional empire and the new, emerging entity— an entity that would survive for another century and a half only at the expense of its traditional institutions and cosmology.

Bibliography

Students interested in further reading on Ottoman history will find several reference and general survey works indispensable, especially since there is as yet no comprehensive history of the Ottomans available in English. Bernard Lewis, *et al.* (eds.), *The Encyclopaedia of Islam*, rev. ed. (Leiden, Neth.: E. J. Brill, 1960–), contains articles embodying recent scholarship by recognized scholars. The articles "Bursa," "Ciftlik," and "Ghulam," all by Halil Inalcik, the leading Ottoman historian, are pertinent examples. Equally rewarding is P. M. Holt, *et al.* (eds.), *The Cambridge History of Islam*, 2 vols. (Cambridge, Eng.: Cambridge University Press, 1970). The contribution by Halil Inalcik is invaluable. Dorothy M. Vaughn, *Europe and the Turk: A Pattern of Alliances 1350–1700* (Liverpool, Eng.: Liverpool University Press, 1954), is a masterful summary of the empire's relations with the West. It is matched by the treatment of internal events in Bernard Lewis, *The Emergence of Modern Turkey*, 2nd ed. (Oxford, Eng.: Oxford University Press, 1968). Works directly concerned with the material as discussed in this book are listed below.

Chapter 1   From Emirate to Empire

Arnakis, G. G. "Gregory Palamas Among the Turks and Documents of His Captivity as Historical Sources." *Speculum*, Vol. 26 (1951), pp. 104–118.

Atiya, Aziz S. *The Crusade of Nicopolis*. London: Methuen, 1934.

Cahen, Claude. *Pre-Ottoman Turkey*. J. Jones-Williams (tr.). New York: Taplinger, 1968.

Hess, Andrew C. "The Evolution of the Ottoman Seaborne Empire in the Age of the Oceanic Discoveries, 1453–1525." *American Historical Review*, Vol. LXXV, (December 1970), pp. 1889–1919.

*Holt, P. M. *Egypt and the Fertile Crescent, 1516–1922: A Political History*. Ithaca, N.Y.: Cornell University Press, 1966.

*Available in paperback.

Inalcik, Halil. "Ottoman Methods of Conquest." *Studia Islamica,* Fas. II (1954), pp. 103–129.

Merriman, Roger Bigelow. *Suleiman the Magnificent 1520–1566.* Cambridge, Mass.: Harvard University Press, 1944.

Riggs, Charles T. (tr.). *History of Mehmed the Conqueror.* Princeton, N.J.: Princeton University Press, 1954.

*Runciman, Sir Steven. *The Fall of Constantinople, 1453.* Cambridge, Eng.: Cambridge University Press, 1969.

*Wittek, Paul. *The Rise of the Ottoman Empire.* London: Royal Asiatic Society, 1938.

Chapter 2   Ottoman Society and Institutions

Alderson, Anthony D. *The Structure of the Ottoman Dynasty.* Oxford, Eng.: Clarendon Press, 1956.

*Andric, Ivo. *The Bridge on the Drina.* Lovett F. Edward (tr.). New York: Signet, New American Library, 1967.

Gibb, H. A. R. and Bowen, Harold. *Islamic Society and the West.* Vol. 1, pts. 1 and 2. London: Oxford University Press, 1950–57.

Lewis, Bernard. *Istanbul and the Civilization of the Ottoman Empire.* Norman, Okla.: University of Oklahoma Press, 1963.

Lewis, Geoffrey L. (tr.). *The Balance of Truth.* London: Allen and Unwin, 1957.

Lybyer, Albert Howe. *The Government of the Ottoman Empire in the Time of Suleiman the Magnificent.* Cambridge, Mass.: Harvard University Press, 1913.

Miller, Barnette. *The Palace School of Muhammad the Conqueror.* Cambridge, Mass.: Harvard University Press, 1941.

Thomas, Lewis V. and Frye, Richard. *The United States and Turkey and Iran.* Cambridge, Mass.: Harvard University Press, 1951.

Stavrianos, Leften S. *The Balkans Since 1453.* New York: Holt, Rinehart, and Winston, 1958.

Wickens, G. M. (tr.). *The Nasirean Ethics by Nasid ad-Din Tusi.* London: Allen and Unwin, 1964.

Wright, Walter Livingston, Jr. (tr.). *Ottoman Statecraft: The Book of Counsel for Vezirs and Governors.* Princeton, N.J.: Princeton University Press, 1935.

Chapter 3   The Post-Suleimanic Age

Abou-El-Haj, Rifa'at A., "Ottoman Diplomacy at Karlowitz." *Journal of the American Oriental Society,* Vol. 87 (December 1967), pp. 498–512.

*Allen, W. E. D. *Problems of Turkish Power in the Sixteenth Century.* London: Central Asian Research Centre, 1963.

Barker, Thomas M. *Double Eagle and Crescent, Vienna's Second Turkish Siege and its Historical Setting.* Albany, N.Y.: State University of New York Press, 1967.

*Bodman, Herbert L., Jr. *Political Factions in Aleppo, 1760–1826.* Chapel Hill, N.C.: University of North Carolina Press, 1963.

Hess, Andrew C. "The Moriscos: An Ottoman Fifth Column in Sixteenth-Century Spain." *American Historical Review,* Vol. LXXIV (October 1968), p. 1–25.

Kurat, A. N. "The Ottoman Empire under Mehmed IV," *The New Cambridge Modern History,* Vol. 5, pp. 500–518. Cambridge, Eng.: Cambridge University Press, 1961.

McNeill, William H. *Europe's Steppe Frontier 1500–1800.* Chicago, Ill.: University of Chicago Press, 1964.

Pallis, Alexander. *In the Days of the Janissaries.* London: Hutchinson, 1951.

Parry, V. J. "The Ottoman Empire 1566–1617." *The New Cambridge Modern History,* Vol. 3, pp. 347–376. Cambridge, Eng.: Cambridge University Press, 1968.

Sumner, B. H. *Peter the Great and the Ottoman Empire.* Oxford, Eng.: Blackwell, 1949.

Chapter 4   Ottoman Consciousness

Itzkowitz, Norman, "Eighteenth-Century Ottoman Realities." *Studia Islamic,* Fas. XVI (1962), pp. 73–94.

Itzkowitz, Norman and Mote, Max. *Mubadele: An Ottoman-Russian Exchange of Ambassadors.* Chicago, Ill.: University of Chicago Press, 1970.

Lewis, Bernard. "Ottoman Observers of Ottoman Decline." *Islamic Studies,* Vol. 1 (March 1962), pp. 71–87.

Lewis, Bernard. "Some Reflections on the Decline of the Ottoman Empire." *Studia Islamic,* Fas. IX (1958), pp. 111–127.

Lockhart, Laurence. *The Fall of the Safavi Dynasty and the Afghan Occupation of Persia.* Cambridge, Eng.: Cambridge University Press, 1958.

Naff, Thomas. "Reform in the Conduct of Ottoman Diplomacy in the Reign of Selim III, 1789–1807." *Journal of the American Oriental Society,* Vol. 83 (September 1963), pp. 295–315.

*Rosenthal, Erwin I. J. *Political Thought in Medieval Islam: An Introductory Outline.* Cambridge, Eng.: Cambridge University Press, 1962.

*Rosenthal, Franz (tr.). *Ibn Khaldun: The Muqaddimah: An Introduction to History*. Abridged and edited by N. J. Dawood. Princeton, N.J.: Princeton University Press, 1969.

Shaw, Stanford J. *Between Old and New. The Ottoman Empire under Sultan Selim III 1789–1807*. Cambridge, Mass.: Harvard University Press, 1971.

Shay, Mary Lucille. *The Ottoman Empire from 1720 to 1734 as Revealed in Despatches of the Venetian Baili*. Urbana, Ill.: University of Illinois Press, 1944.

Chronology

1299–1326	Osman I
1301	Battle of Baphaeon; key victory over the Byzantines
1326–1362	Orhon
1326	Bursa captured
1331	Nicaea (Iznik) falls
1337	Nicomedia (Izmid) falls
1354	Gallipoli taken
1361	Adrianople (Edirne) falls
1362–1389	Murad I
1389	Battle of Kossovo; Ottomans victorious, but Murad I slain
1389–1402	Bajazet I
1394	Title of Sultan of Rum granted to Bajazet I
1402	Battle of Ankara; Timur captures Bajazet I
1402–1413	The Interregnum
1403	Death of Bajazet I in captivity
1413–1421	Mohammed I
1421–1451	Murad II
1444	Abdication of Murad II; Battle of Varna
1451–1481	Mohammed the Conqueror
1453	Constantinople falls
1473	Uzun Hasan defeated
1475	The Crimea comes under Ottoman suzerainty
1481–1512	Bajazet II
1512–1520	Selim I
1514	Battle of Chaldiran; Selim defeats Shah Ismail
1516–1517	Syria and Egypt taken
1520–1566	Suleiman the Magnificent
1521	Belgrade falls
1522	Rhodes captured
1529	First siege of Vienna
1533–1535	Suleiman's first eastern campaign
1548–1549	Suleiman's second eastern campaign
1555	Peace of Amasya with the Safavids
1566–1574	Selim II
1570–1571	Invasion and capture of Cyprus
1571	Battle of Lepanto
1574	Tunis retaken

1574–1595	Murad III
1578	Start of long eastern campaign
1580	Battle of Alcazar
1590	Peace with the Safavids
1593–1606	War with the Hapsburgs ended by the Treaty of Zsitva-Torok
1595–1603	Mohammed III
1595–1610	*Celâli* revolts
1603–1617	Ahmed I; succession passes to his brother after him
1617–1618	Mustafa I
1618–1622	Osman II; assassinated in janissary uprising
1623–1640	Murad IV
1639	Peace with the Safavids
1640–1648	Ibrahim I; deposed and then strangled
1646–1687	Mohammed IV
1656	Lemnos and Tenedos fall to the Venetians
1656–1661	Grand Vizier Mohammed Kuprili
1657–1658	Abaza Hasan Pasha leads revolt
1657	Lemnos and Tenedos recaptured by the Ottomans
1661–1676	Grand Vizier Fazil Ahmed Kuprili
1664	Battle of St. Gotthard; Ottomans defeated
1669	Crete falls
1676–1683	Grand Vizier Kara Mustafa Pasha, brother-in-law of Fazil Ahmed
1683	Second siege of Vienna
1691–1695	Ahmed II
1691	Battle of Slankamen; Mustafa Kuprili killed
1695–1703	Mustafa II
1697	Battle of Senta; disastrous defeat for the Ottomans
1699	Treaty of Karlowitz
1703–1730	Ahmed III; the Tulip Period
1711	Peter the Great defeated
1715	The Morea retaken
1736–1739	Ottomans victorious over the Australians and the Russians; Belgrade retaken
1757–1774	Mustafa III
1768–1774	War with Russia
1774	Treaty of Küchük Kainarja
1789–1807	Selim III; era of reforms initiated

Glossary

akcha	Ottoman coin.
askeri	The Ottoman military class.
ayan	"Notables." Distinguished inhabitant of city or town who exercised local political power.
beglerbeglik	The office of beglerbeg and the region under his command.
celâlîs	Brigands who ravaged the Anatolian countryside, especially in the period from 1595 to 1610.
chikma	"Graduation" or promotion procedure within the Inner and Outer Services.
devshirme	Levy of Christian youths.
ghulam	"Young man," used in the sense of a young slave specially trained for the sultan's service.
hacegân	Upper bracket of the Ottoman bureaucracy.
has	A grant with an income in excess of 100,000 akchas yearly. The grant was usually associated with the office rather than the holder.
kafes	Special apartments set aside in the palace for the royal princes.
kanun	Law or statute. A regulation issued by the sultan based on his authority rather than on religious law.
kanun-name	Codification of *kanuns,* frequently associated with the list of regulations governing a province.
millet	Organized religious minority.
reaya	Subjects of the sultan, usually designating the peasantry.
reisülküttab	Chief of the scribes in the bureaucracy.
sanjak	Basic territorial administrative unit.
sekban	Irregular soldier equipped with firearms.
Sipahi	Cavalryman.
Sunnah	Accepted Islamic practice based on the life of Muhammad and his companions.
tahrir	Cadastral survey.
timar	Grant for an income derived from agricultural taxation for the support generally of members of the provincial cavalry.
timariot	Holder of a timar, provincial cavalryman.
valide	Mother of the sultan.
wakf	A pious foundation.
zaim	Holder of a timar with an income in excess of 20,000 akchas a year.
zeamet	A timar granted to a *zaim.*

Index

Abaza Hasan Pasha, 79
Abbas I, Shah, 71
Abbas, II, Shah, 72–73
Abu Bakr, Caliph, 31, 69
Ahmed I, Sultan, 72–73
Ahmed II, Sultan, 83
Ahmed III, Sultan, 103
Ahmed Ghazi, 7
Albania, 24, 43, 44–46
Alcazar, Battle of, 68
Algeria, 35, 66
Alp Arslan, Sultan, 6–7
Amasya, 22, 29, 31, 36, 70, 73
Anatolia, 6–27, 39, 70, 77–79, 98
   central, 22, 27, 32, 42
   east, 27, 31, 32, 68
   inflation, 94–95
   population growth, 93–94
   west, 42
Assassinations, 16, 19, 75, 76, 79, 82
Augustus III of Poland, 108
Austria and the Austrians, 35, 81–84, 97, 100, 103, 107

Baghdad, 5, 20, 35, 71, 73
Bajazet I, the Thunderbolt, Sultan, 16–21, 43, 68
Bajazet II, Sultan, 29–31, 53
Baki (poet), 36
Balkans, 12–19, 22, 31, 42, 50, 85, 98
Banat of Temsevar, 84
Belgrade, 23, 81, 83, 103
Black Sea, 9, 13, 26–27, 30, 64, 70–71, 83
Booty, 6, 11–12, 20–21, 25, 39, 49, 82, 95
Bosnia, 15–16, 26, 83
Boynuyarali Mohammed Pasha, Grand Vizier, 77
Bulgaria, 14–16
Bursa, 11, 13, 22, 23–24, 58, 98
Byzantines, 6–12, 17, 19, 23, 26, 48

Careers
   bureaucracy, 95, 100, 104

Careers (*continued*)
  influence of conquest, 95
  military-administrative, 104
  mobility, 104
  religion, 95
  specialization, 59–60
Caspian Sea, 64, 70–71
Cem, 29, 31
Chandarli Halil Pasha, Grand Vizier, 23–25, 53
Charles V, 4, 34, 65
Christians, 6, 11–12, 21, 30, 34, 41 46, 58–59, 66–68, 71–72, 82, 84,
  youth conscription, 49–50, 53
Class distinctions, 59–60, 86
  askeri, 40–41, 44, 46–47, 58–61, 88–90
  reaya, 40, 58–59, 61, 88–92, 99, 102–103
Comenus, Alexis, 9
Commerce and trade, 4–5, 23, 26–27, 35, 69, 71, 94–95
Communication, public, 66, 96, 104–106, 109
Constantinople, 3–4, 6, 8–10, 18–19, 22, 24–25, 27–28, 37, 97–98
Crete, 75–76, 79, 95
Crimea, 27, 64–65, 71, 84, 103
Croatia, 71, 84
Crusades, 8–9, 12, 66–67
Cyprus, 66–67, 95

Danube River, 19, 72, 76, 83
Devlet Giray, khan of the Crimea, 64
Devshirme system, 49–51, 53, 60–61, 89, 94, 104
Don Juan of Austria, 66–67
Don Sebastian of Portugal, 68
Ducas, Constantine, 6
Dushan, Stephen, 13–14

Ebüssund, sheikh ul-Islam, 58
Edirne, 12–13, 22, 24, 51, 98
Education, 27–28, 58–61
  apprentice training, 57
  palace schools, 60, 77, 100, 104
  religion, 11, 58, 60, 96
Egypt, 20, 27, 33, 65–66, 76
Europe, 12–14, 16, 18, 22–24, 26, 29–30, 34–35, 48–49, 66–68, 71–72, 79–85, 96–98, 104–109

France and the French, 19, 105, 108
  alliance with Ottomans, 34
Frederick Augustus, Elector of Saxony, King of Poland, 84

George II Rakoczy, Prince of Transylvania, 80
Ghazis, 6–12, 15–16, 18–21, 23, 30, 38, 63, 65, 67, 71, 81, 98
Ghulam system, 20–21, 49–53, 56, 91
   career assignments, 52–54
   education, 50–52
   janissary corps, 49–50, 91
Gladstone, William, 85
Government
   central, 17–18, 20–21, 26, 47–49, 54, 58–59, 66, 73, 92–95
   divans, 54–55, 64, 77
   fiscal policies, 20, 28, 47–49, 56, 59, 92–96
   personnel, 55–56
   philosophy of rule, 38–39
   provincial, 26, 41–49, 50, 53, 67, 92–93, 95
   structure, 38–39, 54–58
   tahrirs, 42–45, 48
Grand viziers, 29, 53–55, 64, 76–80, 99–100, 102–04, 107
Greece and the Greeks, 10–12, 24, 26, 35, 38, 59, 83, 104–05
Gregory Palamas, Bishop of Salonika, 39

Hapsburgs, 34–35, 37, 65–68, 71, 82–84, 92, 100
Holy League, 82–83
Holy wars, 22, 25–26, 30, 34, 37
Hungary, 15, 18, 22–23, 26, 30, 36, 71–72, 80, 84
Hunyadi, János, 23
Husrev Aga, 77
Husrev Molla, 23

Ibn Khaldun, *Muqaddimah*, 100–101
Ibrahim, Sultan, 74–75
Indian Ocean, 33, 35
Isa, 22
Islam, 4–5, 27–28, 32, 35, 51, 58
   converts, 46, 51–52
   cultural isolation, 96–97, 104–07
   High Islamic tradition, 5, 8, 15, 17, 24, 38, 60, 87, 98–99
   Islamic millenium, 97
   religious law, 15, 38–39, 50, 55, 78
   See also Government; Muslims; Seljuks
Ismail, Shah, 30–32, 69
Ismail II, Shah, 70
Istanbul, 3–4, 27–28, 31–32, 36, 50–51, 58, 64–65, 69–70,
   75–77, 79, 82, 92–94, 97–99
Iznik, 9, 10–11

Janissary system, 20, 24–26, 29–30, 32, 61, 70, 90–92, 100
Jews, 34, 59

John VI Cantacuzenus, Emperor, 11–12

Kara Mustafa Pasha, 81–82, 102
Karaman ibn Musa Sufi, 9
Karamanids, 9, 15–16, 19, 22–23, 27, 29
Karlowitz, Treaty of, 84, 100, 103
Katib Chelebi, *The Guide to Practice for the Rectification of Defects*, 99–102, 105–06
Kenan Pasha, 76
Khair ed-Din Barbarossa, 35, 65
Khan of the Golden Horde, 27
Konya, 8, 11, 15, 18–19, 29
Kösem (grandmother of Mohammed IV), 74–75
Kraljević, Marko, 14
Kritovoulos (Greek historian), 27
Kuprili, Fazil Ahmed, Grand Vizier, 80
Kuprili, Hussein Amcazade, Grand Vizier, 84, 100–101
Kuprili, Mohammed, Grand Vizier, 77–81, 99

Lascarids, 9–10
Lascaris, Theodore, Emperor, 9
Legal system
    personal status, 59
    religion, 20, 25, 43, 55, 79
    sheik ul-Islam, role of, 57–58
    "tower of justice," 57
Lepanto, Battle of, 35, 67, 76
Louis XIV of France, 82–83
Lutfi Pasha, Grand Vizier, 53–54

Mahmud Pasha, Grand Vizier, 53
Mamluks, 20, 27, 30–31, 33
Mecca, 33, 35, 98, 101
Medina, 33, 35, 98
Mediterranean area, 9, 30, 34–36, 37, 63, 65–68, 76
Michael VIII Palaeologus, Emperor, 10
Military establishment
    cavalry, 18, 33, 45–46, 90, 97
    modern weapons, 92–93
    navy, 30, 33, 35, 65, 67, 76, 79
    Sipahis of the Porte, 91, 93
    transportation logistics, 97–99
Millets, 59
Mohammed I, Sultan, 22, 43
Mohammed II, the Conqueror, Sultan, 4, 23–29, 31, 41, 51, 53–54, 58, 68, 98
Mohammed III, Sultan, 74

Mohammed IV, Sultan, 75, 81–82
Mohammed Raghip, Grand Vizier, 104
Mohammed Sokollu Pasha, Grand Vizier, 64, 77
Mongols, 19–20
Morea, 17, 26, 31, 103
Moriscos, 66, 68
Muhammad, Prophet, 6, 30–31, 59, 100–101
Murad I, Sultan, 13–15, 16, 20, 42, 49
Murad II, Sultan, 22–23, 31, 43
Murad III, Sultan, 67–68
Murad IV, Sultan, 73–74, 77
Musa, 21
Muslims, 3–5, 18–21, 25–26, 34, 39–40, 56, 58–59, 61, 64, 67, 69, 87, 96, 105
Mustafa I, Sultan, 74
Mustafa II, Sultan, 83
Mustafa III, Sultan, 99
Mustafa Kemal Atatürk, 38
Mutasim, al-, Caliph, 49

Nabi (poet), 28
Nasireddin Tusi, *The Nasirean Ethics*, 39, 58–59
Nedim (poet), 3
Nicholas II, Tsar of Russia, 63
Nomads, 4–5, 40, 92
Non-Muslims, 6, 26, 29, 34, 40, 47, 58–61, 66, 98
North Africa, 33, 35–36, 37, 63, 65, 67–68

Orhon, 11–12
Osman, 4, 10–11, 38
Osman II, Sultan, 74
Ottoman Empire
  capitals, 98
  hereditary benefits, 12, 38, 46, 59–60, 88–89, 104
  intellectuals,27, 37, 87–107
  justification for conquest, 69
  New Order, 109
  Ottoman Way, 60, 99
  social unrest, 17, 71–73, 79, 92–96

Palaeologi, 10, 23, 26
Persia, 5, 9, 20, 48, 64, 69–73, 95, 98
  Safavids, 30–32, 35–36, 68–70, 73, 83, 98
Peter the Great, 83–84, 103
Philip II of Spain, 67–68
Poland, 79–84, 108
Pope Innocent XI, 83

Portugal and the Portuguese, 33–35, 67–68, 98

Romanus IV Diogenes, 6
Rumeli, 42, 51, 57–58
Russia and the Russians, 27, 35, 63–64, 83–84, 103, 107

Salonika, 23
Sari Mehmed Pasha, *Book of Counsel for Vezirs and Governors,*
    88–89
Selim I the Grim, Sultan, 31–33, 54, 70, 91
Selim II, Sultan, 36–37, 66–67
Selim III, Sultan, 108–09
Seljuks, 5–10, 15, 32, 48–49
Serbia, 14–16, 18, 22–23, 26
Shahrukh, 22
Shi'ites, 30–32, 68–70, 72, 98
Shirvan, 70
Shishman of Bulgaria, 14, 16, 18
Sigismund, King of Hungary, 19, 22
Sinan Pasha, 4
Slaves, slavery, 20–21, 24–25, 29, 41, 45–46, 49, 53, 58, 90
Spain, 30, 34, 66–67
Suleiman the Magnificent, Sultan, 4, 12, 34–37, 44, 46, 51, 53,
    56, 58–59, 61, 64–65, 68–70, 73, 79, 81, 89, 91, 95, 97, 107
Suleiman II, Sultan, 83
Suleiman ibn Kutulmush, 7–8
Sultan, role of, 3–4, 18–23, 28–29, 32, 38, 43, 46–48, 50–52,
    54, 57, 59, 61, 64–65, 67, 73, 78–79, 83, 87–99, 103
    succession, 31, 74–75
Sunnites, 31, 99

Tabriz, 32–33, 35, 71–72, 97
Tamasp I, Shah, 70
Tamerlane, *see* Timur Lenk
Tartars, 29, 64, 80, 83, 103
Timars, timariots, 5, 14–15, 17–18, 20–21, 28, 40–48, 50, 53,
    55, 61, 67, 69, 77, 89–90, 92–93, 96
    Christian 41, 58
Timur Lenk, 19–21, 68, 97
Trade routes, 35, 64, 70, 94
Transylvania, 23, 79–80, 84
Trebizond, 9, 26, 31
Tughrul Beg, 5
Turcomans, 4–7, 9–10, 19, 26–27, 31, 70
Turhan (mother of Mohammed IV), 75–78
Turkey and the Turks, 11, 20–22, 24, 38, 51, 81, 85

Ulema, 25, 57, 59, 96
Umur, Bey of Izmir, 12, 43
Uzun Hasan, 27, 68

Vasco da Gama, 31, 33
Vasvar, Treaty of, 80–81
Venice and the Venetians, 18, 22, 26, 30, 32, 35, 67, 75–76, 79, 83–84
Viziers, 47, 54, 107
    See also Grand viziers
Volga River, 35, 64–65

Women's income, 45

Zaganos Pasha, 24–25

A NOTE
ON THE TYPE

This book is set in Electra, a Linotype face designed by W. A. Dwiggins. This face cannot be classified as either modern or old-style. It is not based on any historical model, nor does it echo any particular period or style. It avoids the extreme contrasts between thick and thin elements that mark most modern faces, and attempts to give a feeling of fluidity, power, and speed.

Composed by Cherry Hill Composition, Pennsauken, New Jersey. Printed, and bound by The Colonial Press, Inc. Clinton, Massachusetts.